THE OTHER NIETZSCHE

SUNY Series in Philosophy
Edited by George R. Lucas, Jr.

The Other Nietzsche

JOAN STAMBAUGH

State University of New York Press

Published by
State University of New York Press, Albany

© 1994 State University of New York

Printed in the United States of America

For information, address State University of New York Press,
State University Plaza, Albany, N.Y., 12246

Production by Cathleen Collins
Marketing by Dana Yanulavich

Library of Congress Cataloging-in-Publication Data

Stambaugh, Joan, 1932–
    The other Nietzsche / Joan Stambaugh.
       p. cm. — (SUNY series in philosophy)
    Includes bibliographical references and index.
    ISBN 0–7914–1699–2 (hc) — ISBN 0–7914–1700–X (pb)
    1. Nietzsche, Friedrich Wilhelm, 1844–1900. I. Title.
II. Series.
B3317.S66 1993
193—dc20

                                    93–18455
                                       CIP

10 9 8 7 6 5 4 3 2

To Henry Bugbee

Contents

Prefatory Note

Everyone seems to have his or her own Nietzsche. There
are various versions of Nietzsche belonging to literary
criticism and also to musicologists. There is the Nietzsche distortion perpetrated by the Nazis. There was a
lot of pre-Kaufmann nonsense about the Nietzsche who
was mad from the outset and produced nothing but the
ravings of a madman. More recently and more philosophically, the two main continental interpretations have
been expressed by the French, neo-Freudian, and Derridian line and the German, Heideggerian line that sees
in Nietzsche the completion of the history of metaphysics. These two interpretations are valid in varying
degrees. What this book is trying to explore is a Nietzsche relatively untouched by most of these interpretations. It is not the whole of Nietzsche by any means; but
it is there. I shall call the other Nietzsche: *Nietzsche the
poetic mystic.*

Acknowledgments

The author wishes to acknowledge the following philosophy journals and books in which these chapters first appeared:

"On Creativity and Decadence" under the title, "Nietzsche on Creativity and Decadence," *Philosophy Today* (Summer 1977): 162–167.

"Thoughts on Pity and Revenge," *Nietzsche-Studien*, vol. 1 (Berlin: Walter de Gruyter, 1972), pp. 27–35.

"Thoughts on a *Nachlass* Fragment" as "Thoughts on a *Nachlass* Fragment from Nietzsche," *Nietzsche-Studien*, vol 6 (Berlin: Walter de Gruyter, 1977), pp. 195–204.

"*Amor dei* and *Amor fati:* Spinoza and Nietzsche," reprinted from *Studies in Nietzsche and the Judaeo-Christian Tradition*, edited by James C. O'Flaherty. Published for the North Carolina Studies in the Germanic Languages and Literatures Series. Copyright © 1985 by The University of North Carolina Press.

"The Innocence of Becoming" as "Thoughts on the Innocence of Becoming" *Nietzsche-Studien*, vol. 14 (Berlin: Walter de Gruyter, 1985), pp. 164–178.

"The Other Nietzsche," chapter 9 of the current work, under the same title in *Nietzsche and Asian Thought* (Chicago: University of Chicago Press, 1991). Reprinted by permission.

CHAPTER ONE

Nietzsche Today

This past summer I attended a conference in Cerisy-la-Salle, France, on the topic of Nietzsche Today? (Nietzsche aujourd'hui?). The title of the conference was formulated as a question and it remained, at least for me, a question throughout the meeting. I have seldom witnessed such a disparity of points of view from which to approach a thinker. This disparity left me at the end of the conference with a somewhat puzzled question mark instead of some kind of focus on the kind of interest in Nietzsche predominant in France and Germany today.

I should like to deal very briefly with a few of the French speakers, then touch upon the German speakers, and conclude with some remarks of my own on the subject of Nietzsche today. These remarks will take the form of questioning his impact on the possible direction of *philosophy* today.

The topics the French speakers chose centered around such questions as Nietzsche's relation to art, teleology, culture and philology. I found some of these papers rather foreign to my own way of thinking, particularly when such Nietzschean concepts as eternal recurrence were interpreted in a pseudo-Freudian manner. Perhaps one of the most interesting and thought-provoking papers was on dissimulation, by Lacoue-Labarthe, who linked Nietzsche, particularly in *Thus Spoke Zarathustra*, to the late Schelling in his attempt to escape the confines of simple logic by telling tales or sagas in areas where nothing could be proved or demonstrated. In the late Schelling, myth or *mythos* replaces *logos* in realms that defy rational proof or explanation; as in, for instance, *The Ages of the World*, where Schelling makes the bold attempt to *tell* of the origination of the world.

To turn to the German tradition, with which I am far more familiar, a day was scheduled to discuss Heidegger's interpretation of Nietzsche, but such discussion, insofar as it took place at all, cropped up more informally and sporadically throughout the conference without ever becoming a main topic. Heidegger's interpretation of Nietzsche as the last figure of metaphysics, whereby the Will to Power is the *essence* of all things and eternal recurrence is the *existence* of all things, was treated with a sort of respectful and cautious distance.

Karl Löwith spoke of Nietzsche's completion of atheism, showing that with Nietzsche the concept "world" ceased to have any connection with God or any possible kind of transcendence. The philosophical relation to be thought had become that of man and world.

Finally, Eugen Fink, who has his own philosophical concept of "world" quite independent of Nietzsche, made the distinction between what is *within* the world (*das Binnenweltliche*) and the world itself. By abolishing the distinction between Being and the world, between Being and becoming, Nietzsche had abandoned ontology and attempted to think pure becoming devoid of a substrate of Being.

Instead of trying to develop further what went on in that conference—a conference set in a beautiful Chateau in Normandy a few miles away from a beach where, when the tide was in, the swimming was magnificent; and, when the tide was out, one stared glumly and disconsolately at miles of wet, oozing mud—I should like to present a few thoughts of my own on the topic of Nietzsche Today?

What I should like to talk about briefly is the effect that Nietzsche's thought has had and could have on philosophy. I shall select two of his most controversial and influential ideas: (1) the absolute loss of transcendence (God is dead); and (2) the dethroning of reason as man's most characteristic and cherished faculty. It would seem that these are both "negative" ideas with no positive content—ideas denying nearly a whole historical tradition of Western thinking. That tradition goes back to Plato's correlation of reason (*nous*) with the highest transcendence, the Idea of Good, to which reason alone had access. In their various historical transformations, reason, the highest transcendence, and the correlation between the two have remained decisive throughout the development of philosophy. After a discussion of just what about these ideas Nietzsche is specifically negating, I should like to ask about a new, affirmative direction for philosophy arising out of this negation, not just in spite of it.

Nietzsche's proclamation that God is dead is really more of a philosophical statement than a specifically antireligious, atheistic one. What he is denying most of all is a transcendent world ("backworld," as he calls it) or realm. Christianity is "Platonism for the people"; and it is, thus, Platonism in his understanding of that term which Nietzsche is primarily denying.

Why should an attack on Platonism have any particular impact for thinkers today? Platonism has undergone many radical transformations and was a target of attack long before Nietzsche. The Platonic forms, for instance, became Ideas in the mind of God with the advent of Christianity. Their existence was denied altogether by the nominalists of the Medieval period who stated that universals were a mere breath of air (i.e., they had only a verbal status, hardly an ontological one.)

Nietzsche's denial of transcendence is more radical than any previous polemic against Platonism. Under the name of Platonism, Nietzsche is attacking *anything at all that transcends man:* God, ground of the world, first cause, highest being, suprasensible being, all being in general in the sense of that which is changeless. He is attacking the *philosophical* concept of God as it has appeared in Western thought. There is nothing beyond man.

This means that there is nothing beyond man in the sense that there is no God of substance or world beyond him. Accordingly, for Nietzsche, the word *transcendence* cannot have its traditional meaning of naming some kind of being but, rather, acquires the meaning of *what man does;* or, rather, has never yet done but *could do.* Nietzsche states repeatedly in *Thus Spoke Zarathustra:* "Man is something that has to be surpassed." I believe Nietzsche is striving for a new meaning of transcendence. This new meaning is the shift from thinking transcendence as something beyond man to thinking it as man's activity in transcending his human, all too human condition.

Of course, Nietzsche is hardly the first thinker who wanted to "improve" man. But he saw ominous possibilities in man to a perhaps unprecedented degree—possibilities epitomized in the figure of the last man in *Thus Spoke Zarathustra* who hops around like the inexterminable ground flea, blinking and exulting in the fact that he has found happiness. The small man exemplifies an intolerable aspect of human existence just as it is, lacking any possible dimension of self-overcoming or transcendence. The two attitudes that are Zarathustra's greatest danger, pity (*Mitleid*), and nausea or disgust (*Ekel*), arise in the face of the almost overwhelming pervasiveness of man's smallness, arise from the fact that "never yet has there been a overman."

We seek, if not some*thing* beyond existence, a *way* leading above existence just as it is. Nietzsche is saying that we have not yet found that way because we have been looking for something *outside ourselves*, even outside our "world." We have not even found out yet what or who *we* are, what man is. "Man is the still undetermined animal."

This leads back to Nietzsche's other major thought to be discussed here—his attack on the supremacy of reason. We must ask what is to be the nature and center of man, if not reason; and, in this connection, we must first ask what in man has to be surpassed.

Man is something that has to be surpassed. Because he is no longer to be surpassed by someone or something already above and superior to him, he must surpass himself. He must, so to speak, bring about his own self-transcendence. How is this possible?

Most of Nietzsche's writings speak of the many facets of man that are to be overcome. They abound with polemic against mediocrity, hypocrisy, herd morality, passivity, and so on. These are qualities that are sheerly negative, ultimately stemming from some form of weakness or powerlessness. Nietzsche's critique of reason, on the other hand, is by no means simply a *rejection* of reason but, rather, a *caution* against the vast overestimation of reason that has occurred in Western philosophy. Some of Nietzsche's criticism of the renowned faculty of reason lands in a swampy glorification of the instincts and the senses, enticing us to believe that the animal is better off without the rational. But I do not believe that this represents the most interesting and the most provocative level of his thinking, aside from the fact that Nietzsche himself counterbalances and corrects himself on this issue.

I should, rather, like to focus on Nietzsche's analysis of man's *use* of reason. In other words, Nietzsche might not quarrel with Aristotle's definition of man as the animal who has *logos*, the animal rationale, but he would probably not accept it as truly definitive in any ultimate sense. The issue is not so much the fact that man is the animal who has reason but, rather, the question of what he has done and what he will do with that reason. In many of his writings, Nietzsche considers reason more of a tool than a guide. The question then becomes, What guides reason?

What Nietzsche has shown rather brilliantly is what has guided reason up to now, while parading reason as its supposed champion and leader. Apart from his statements, sometimes extremely general and sometimes specific to the point of turning into a brand of home-style, do-it-yourself physiology, about the dominance of the senses and the instincts, Nietzsche's philosophically most interesting and fruitful anaylsis of this hidden guide lies in his statements about *ressentiment* and the spirit of revenge. These statements are not of merely "psychological" significance, but have a truly "ontological" status. In fact, I should like to suggest at the end of this chapter that one of Nietzsche's greatest legacies to philosophy today is having made this distinction of the ontological and the psychological—or however else one wants to formulate it—questionable without, however, deriving one exclusively from the other or reducing one to the other.

In *Thus Spoke Zarathustra*, Nietzsche states that man's best thinking (*Nachdenken*) up to now has been the spirit of revenge. A major instance of this statement would be man's revenge upon the witness, the killing of God because God watched everything man did. Nietzsche may well be saying that the spirit of revenge created a backworld of transcendence out of dissatisfaction with this world (Nietzsche's understanding of Platonism) and now that this backworld of transcendence has become, so to speak, autonomous and paralyzing in its effect upon man by its constant surveillance, man must kill what he once created. The second act of revenge destroys what the first one produced.

The gist of Nietzsche's analyses of the spirit of revenge seems to be that the essence of revenge is to "create" out of a lack of power. The spirit of revenge stems from *wishing* that things were otherwise (*Wünschbarkeiten*), which is diametrically opposed to *willing* that they *become* otherwise.

If our reason has hitherto been guided by the spirit of revenge, the question now becomes, What is to guide our reason, if reason is essential to us but, by itself, inadequate to be decisive? Instead of wishing things were otherwise, which is characteristic of the spirit of revenge, Nietzsche proposes willing that they become otherwise, something that can stem only from a prior affirmation of things as they are. Any willing that does not stem from affirmation falls back into the spirit of revenge that is unable to enact anything. But the will stemming from an affirmation of life as it is leads to the possibility of willing things to become otherwise. I believe this is a connection between Nietzsche's two fundamental ideas of eternal recurrence and the Will to Power. Briefly stated, an affirmation of life as it is (I am able to affirm my life exactly as it is by my willingness, far rather by my wanting nothing more with my whole being than to live it again) is the condition of the possibility of willing an increase in the fullness and power of things, willing them to become *More*.

The Will to Power offers a dimension of transcendence in Nietzsche's philosophy that is otherwise strictly a philosophy of "immanence." Nietzsche rejects transcendence in its traditional sense as being a powerless wishing for the Other in every form, whether for a God as the epitome of otherness (different from the finite world and the human condition in every respect) or for a being otherwise of life itself. Instead, Nietzsche thinks the possibility of transcendence as man's activity of self-overcoming.

His self-overcoming or self-transcendence is possible only on the power-ful basis of affirmation.

I believe that Nietzsche implicitly places the affirmation of life at the center of man's being. The affirmation of life offers to man the possibility of becoming truly human.

Instead of defining man in terms of his most unique faculty, reason, Nietzsche is groping for a new concept of the "still undetermined animal" in terms of his attitude toward life. We must ask the question, What is an attitude? *Attitude* is not a technical term in philosophy nor is it coined as one by Nietzsche. But the question of one's stance with regard to life is one of Nietzsche's fundamental concerns going back to *The Birth of Tragedy* and even before that. Nietzsche's whole innovative conception of tragedy arose out of his question, How did the Greeks bear the terror and horror of existence? His answer was a lifelong, impassioned rejection of pessimism, also of optimism, and later on of nihilism, all through tragic affirmation. His final root question is, Can I affirm eternal recurrence, can I affirm living my life over and over again just as it is for all "eternity?"

Again we ask, What is an attitude? An attitude is something truly and specifically human that encompasses and includes the whole of human being. An animal does not have an attitude. It simply is the way it is. Man, however, insofar as he is a thinking being, takes on a predominant attitude with regard to the question of life. If he prefers "not to think about it," this is also an attitude, the choice to try to ignore the question of life, a choice that can never quite succeed. An attitude is a kind of "existential choice," to put it in more familiar terms, which has its roots in man's thinking and feeling and even in the inscrutable condition of his body. It, thus, encompasses what has traditionally been called *mind* and *body* and allows room for other factors scarcely thought by our Western tradition.

Nietzsche's groping for a new concept of man, self-surpassing man, the overman, leads him to the monumental and the suprahistorical man in "The Uses and Disadvantages of History for Life," to various types of the higher man in *Thus Spoke Zarathustra*, and finally in the *Genealogy of Morals* to the ascetic, the priest, and above all, the artist.

> It is a sign that one has turned out well when, like Goethe, one clings with ever-greater pleasure and warmth to the "things of this world": For in this way one holds firmly to the greater conception of man, that man becomes the *transfigurer of existence* when he learns to transfigure himself.
>
> What is essential in art remains its *perfection* of existence, its production of perfection and plentitude; art is essentially *affirmation, blessing, deification of existence!*[1]

It would seem that the artist is as close as Nietzsche ever came to expressing what he meant by the overman. And because Nietzsche does not mean art in the museum sense of that word, but rather regards life itself as "art," the artist is the man who shapes and transfigures not only his "material," but above all, himself; and thus, ultimately, life itself. Nietzsche is pointing to a type of human being who *experiences* differently from most of us. The artist is the man *able* to experience and shape a higher dimension of reality.

With the word *able,* the intimate connection between

art and power becomes evident. The German word for *art (Kunst)* is related to the verb *to be able (können)*, and it is the artist for Nietzsche who has the highest possible "ability" or power. The artist could have been the prototype for the third metamorphosis in the three metamorphoses of the spirit in *Thus Spoke Zarathustra*. The spirit changes from the load-bearing camel whose motto is "You shall," to the lion whose motto is "I will," to the child who alone is able to create and say "I can."

When Nietzsche speaks of art as a "deification of existence," he is pointing to the artist as the man who can "deify" existence itself instead of looking beyond it for a meaning. With the death of God (Platonism), man becomes free to *be* transcendence, to be transcending, self-surpassing being. With the death of God, reason ceases to be the supreme truth about man. Nietzsche is close to Kierkegaard here, the Christian thinker who realized that the important thing is not *what* God is, because the paradox that eternity entered time cannot be grasped by our reason. What is supremely and uniquely important is the entire *manner* of the God relationship, the "how," not the "what."

To stop rather than to conclude, I should like to touch upon the remark made earlier about Nietzsche's role with regard to the distinction between the ontological and the psychological. Nietzsche is concerned primarily with the distinction between the "real" and the "apparent" world, which he believes has become untenable with the loss of Platonism. If one equates Nietzsche's "real" world with what has been fundamentally understood as the realm of ontology, of what causes or is responsible for or is the condition of the possibility of our "apparent" world, and if Nietzsche's "apparent" world can be assimilated to what is commonly called the *psychological*, then we are right at the core of Nietzsche's ambiguity and the possible resultant "crisis" of that ambiguity (crisis in the Kantian sense of critique in the *Critique of Pure Reason* of *krinein*, to de-cide something, to *separate* what can be known from what cannot be known). This ambiguity of the ontological and the psychological, terms admittedly foreign to Nietzsche but very much present as real problems in his thinking, is surely the basis for many of the ambiguities and contradictions, for example, in his attempt to explicate his thought of eternal return. His explications defy the attempt to bifurcate that thought neatly into the subject-object split with its divergent connotations for something like an ethics and a physics, and yet they are not wholly free of it. But thinking through the implications of his rejection of the "real" world, the apparent world would cease to be the merely psychological one.

If there is no real world apart from this world of appearance, then no criterion is left on the basis of which one could judge this world to be apparent, illusory, or less real. We have just—this world. The old metaphysical framework of God-world-man is simply abolished. But, instead of saying that we are left with the merely psychological, we are forced to stop and ponder again the question of what or who man is, man no longer defined as the animal rational nor as the *imago dei*, but questioned in his very being as the still undetermined animal.

I do not challenge what is alive now, I challenge several thousands of years. I contradict, and yet I am the opposite of a negative spirit. Starting now there is hope again, I know tasks of such heights that there was no name for them up to now. I am the *joyous messenger* par excellence even though I also always have to be a man of doom. (*Verhängnis*)[2]

CHAPTER TWO

Creativity and Decadence

Creativity and decadence are two ideas that can be related and have been related in many different ways. The possible ways of relating them embrace a whole scale of nuances that might be polarized into the two extremes of saying that either decadence is a necessary condition of creativity, indissolubly linked with it, or else decadence is antithetical to creativity and detrimental to it. As a recent example of the first view, that creativity and decadence belong together, one might mention Thomas Mann, for whom this theme was central throughout his writings. Already in *Tonio Kröger* one finds the statement: Whoever works, does not live; whoever lives, does not work. By *work* Mann means "create," and he is saying that creativity is not indigenous to the normal, healthy, bourgeois state of life. The healthy, nondecadent, normal, blonde-haired, blue-eyed, mostly stupid figures in Mann's writings are perhaps to be envied, especially by their opposite type, but they are not creative. It is the hypersensitive, dark-haired, dark-eyed type who is creative, and his creativity is paid for at the price of some kind of "decadence" in its broad sense, some kind of physical or moral defect. His creativity demands conditions that are inimical to normal bourgeois life. The fact that he then has to be attracted to his opposite, the healthy, uncreative type, only makes things worse. The epitome of the interrelation of creativity and decadence can be found in Mann's version of *Faustus* where creativity, not youth or wisdom, is bought in a pact with the devil. The price paid for this creativity is the utter sacrifice of any real human relationship, of the love for another human being.

I have mentioned Thomas Mann because Nietzsche's influence is strong in his writings—the Faustian figure of Adrian Leverkühn is based largely upon Nietzsche—and because he gave the ideas of creativity and decadence a literary embodiment that it is hard to forget. For Nietzsche himself, these two ideas are central to an analysis, one might even say diagnosis, of Western culture, its predicaments and its possibilities. Creativity and decadence play such a large role in his writings that the most I can do in these remarks is to sketch out the basic philosophical meaning of each and then try to indicate their relationship.

Of the two extremes mentioned, that creativity and decadence belong together or that they exclude each other, Nietzsche is surely closest to the latter alternative. Decadence is not a purely negative concept for Nietzsche, but it is by no means the ultimate condition of creativity. It has its function in removing man from a cowlike kind of existence, but its dangers soon far exceed whatever advantages it has to offer.

What does decadence, *décadence*, mean for Nietzsche? If this concept is to be understood in a philosophical sense, it should be viewed in the context of his basic ideas and, above all, in the light of Nietzsche's most fundamental question of the affirmation of life. Viewed in this perspective, decadence nearly becomes a synonym for nihilism and the loss of meaning through the development of the highest values of morality. It has two aspects: On the one hand, decadence is an expression for the historical fact of what has happened to Western culture. On the other hand, decadence is inevitably rooted in the nature of life as the necessary counterpart of the will to power. Let us examine these two aspects briefly.

For Nietzsche, decadence as a historical fact begins when this life and this world as it is are negated as something that should not be in favor of a realm or world of perfection that, according to him, is a figment of the fanatical moralistic imagination. The roots of this history go all the way back to Euripides and Socrates and find their fatal culmination in Plato and subsequent "Platonism." In the course of development of Greek tragedy, Euripides brought the spectator, that is, consciousness, on the stage and thus removed the living, Dionysian reality of the tragic chorus. His artistic criterion was, according to Nietzsche, the literal-minded taste of the public for whom everything had to be plausible, comprehensible and well within the comfortable confines of the commonplace. Therefore Nietzsche can say that Greek tragedy died by suicide, its greatness and its "creativity" in the sense of going beyond the ordinary were strangled. One can already hear in Nietzsche's *"Jugendwerk," The Birth of Tragedy* (written when he was 24 years old) the echo of his later proclamation, "God is dead."

Along with Euripides, Nietzsche discovers "that other spectator," Socrates, as the true culprit and opponent of creativity. Euripides turns out to be only a mask, not for Apollo or for Dionysos, but for that other deity, Socrates. The old artistically fruitful duality of the Apollonian world of dream and the Dionysian world of intoxication becomes the mutually exclusive antithesis of the Socratic and Dionysian. The Socratic, or consciousness, becomes the (supposedly) "creative" principle and the Dionysian, or instinct, becomes the critical principle. Thus not only are the *elements* of the antithesis changed, from the Dionysian and the Apollonian to the Dionysian and the Socratic, and thus the nature of the antithesis, but the *roles* they play are also reversed. And the whole mysterious and awesome quality of these mythical principles degenerates into a kind of sterile anthropomorphisized psychology. Apollonian intuitions are replaced by cool, paradoxical *thoughts* and Dionysian ecstasy is replaced by fiery *passions*. The Apollonian becomes a shell of logical schematism, the Dionysian becomes naturalistic emotion.

From here it does not take Nietzsche long to go from Socrates and what he is made to represent to Plato and "philosophy" in the sense of a blind faith in logic at the expense of art. Not only is Plato not interested in art and the creative, he fears its effects and bans most of it from his state. Plato is searching for true, immutable reality, and not finding it in this world of becoming, he posits it in the world of being, the "backworld," and proclaims it accessible only to reason. Here and nowhere else lies the crux of what Nietzsche attacks the whole of his life under the name of *decadence*, and especially under the more philosophical, comprehensive, and ominous term *nihilism*. All of his polemic against morality and Christianity, which he defines as "Platonism for the people," goes back to these roots. In the *Twilight of the Idols* he defines *decadence* as "separating the world into a real and an apparent world," and in the *Will to Power* he calls *morality* the "instinct of decadence" and the "terrible instrument of decadence."

To sum up this discussion of the first, and by far the most important, aspect of decadence for Nietzsche, decadence is by no means an isolated, aristocratic phenomenon with *ennui* and the *pleure involuntaire* of a Baudelaire as it accompaniment, but a terrible fact of history. This terrible fact is decadence in the literal sense of that word as a "falling away from" the mainstream of life as it really is.

The rather vague phrase *life as it really is* can be translated into Nietzsche's basic concept of the will to power. This world *is* the will to power and nothing else. Thus what decadence "falls away from" is precisely the will to power, the striving for self-increase that characterizes the nature of everything living. "Survival of the fittest" and "the will for self-preservation" make no sense for Nietzsche because survival, as mere self-maintenance is already decline and decadence. Nor can the basic nature of things be found in a "will to live" (Schopenhauer) because what is alive does not need to will to live and what is not alive cannot will at all. The alternative to decadence is *power*, this somewhat misleading and vastly misunderstood term that Nietzsche was striving to articulate. Nietzsche does not understand power as a domination of other beings and certainly least of all as some kind of Machiavellian political power. The highest power is power over oneself, and this points to the basic meaning of power as "being able," as the splendid "I can" of the artist. I shall briefly come back to the question of power when I get to the question of creativity.

To conclude these remarks on decadence, I should like to return briefly to the other aspect of decadence, decadence as it is inevitably rooted in the nature of life as the necessary counterpart of the will to power. From the preceding remarks, the meaning of this should be fairly evident. To the will to power as self-increase there necessarily belongs a kind of decrease and decline that is not decadence in the sense Nietzsche is attacking, but a simple expression of the fact that life cannot be a pure, unabated crescendo. Thus Nietzsche can say in the *Will to Power* that decadence is nothing to be condemned or fought against because it is a necessary consequence of life and its growth. What Nietzsche is saying in all of his writings is precisely that *everything* must be affirmed that truly belongs to life, not just what we single out as "positive" and "pleasant." You cannot affirm some things and simply leave out others. You must affirm everything, including decadence. What is important is not to get stuck in decadence and decline, but through this very affirmation to get beyond it. If the term *transcendence* has any meaning for Nietzsche, it lies in the act of affirmation.

To turn now to creativity, it is important to try to mention and then set aside in this discussion a certain reverence for "creativity" and the cult of the "genius" that Nietzsche, particularly the early Nietzsche, shares with many late nineteenth century thinkers. This reverence and this cult in general are perhaps a derivative expression for something that lies deeper and that is philosophically more interesting for us here: The growing realization that knowledge is not going to provide an "answer" to the question of life. In general, one can probably say that an interest in creativity is a modern phenomenon that really gains momentum, again, only in the late nineteenth century. The Greeks had no absorbing interest in creativity. They do not even have a word to distinguish the artisan from the sculptor. Both are "artists," the carpenter is as "creative" as the so-called artist. Art or *techne* is a kind of "know-how" and can be applied to any realm of life. One need recall only Plato's ironic description of Ion the rhapsodist who falls asleep whenever anyone recites the work of a poet other than Homer.

Even in the nineteenth century it is perhaps Schelling who first places art and creativity at the apex of human endeavor. In contrast to Hegel for whom art was the lowest step on the final triad of the ladder of absolute Spirit—art, religion, and philosophy—because it never attains the level of the pure concept, Schelling in his *System of Transcendental Idealism* finds art the highest possible union of nature and Spirit, thus more inclusive and "real" than even philosophy.

But Nietzsche's interest in art and creativity hardly coincides with the systematic interest of German Idealism. However, even though his interest is not "systematic" in the special sense of that word which strictly applies only to the German Idealists, Nietzsche sees art as fundamental to life, as the "truly metaphysical activity of man." Instead of attempting to comprehend art as the synthesis of nature and spirit, he simply abandons these problems in their traditional form and concentrates on art not as a sphere of culture, not as a highly specialized, privileged area for the few, but as that activity of man that is most crucial to his life. This sounds very strange. Surely physical needs such as eating and sleeping are crucial to life, work is crucial to life, and in a more abstract sense science is crucial to life in our technological age. But art?

Because Nietzsche is not a "social" philosopher in the sense of a Karl Marx, he is not concerned with the improvement of man's actual material and social condition. He does emphasize the material and sensuous aspects of man as opposed to the German Idealists, but he is not interested in social reform. This leaves him with the basic alternatives of science (not in the specialized sense of the physical sciences, but in the broad sense of the German *Wissenschaft* that includes the sciences of the humanities as well, and was even the name for philosophy in German Idealism) and "art" as what is important for man's condition and what concerns him in his humanity. Plato sought the "truth," the Idea, Nietzsche no longer does. "We have art lest we *perish through the truth*" (*The Will to Power*, No. 822). What does this mean?

For Nietzsche, *there is no truth* in the traditional sense of that word. The world of the will to power is in constant flux, not the undefined, undetermined flux of Heraclitus, but the flux of shifting centers of power that increase and decrease, but never remain the same. True knowledge of this world is impossible, in fact, it is incommensurate with the very nature of the world. "Knowing" is simply a pragmatic *falsification* of the world for the purpose of dealing with it more effectively. Therefore, instead of despairing over the fact that there is no static, finished world to be known, the meaningful activity in this world of flux and the will to power becomes art, shaping this world, giving it meaning and values. The previous institutions and endeavors of man are forms of decadence, they *distort* the world. "Our religion, morality, and philosophy are decadent forms of man. The *countermovement: art*" (*The Will to Power*, No. 794). "The belief that the world as it ought to be *is*, really exists, is a belief of the unproductive who do *not desire to create a world* as it ought to be. They posit it as already available, they seek ways and means of reaching it. 'Will to truth'—*as the impotence of the will to create*" (*The Will to Power*, No. 585).

Therefore the only meaningful way for man to live in a world of the will to power is to create. For *create* Nietzsche uses the German word *schaffen*, which means to do something, accomplish something, to work, rather than the narrower word *schöpfen,* which more exactly corresponds to creating. This is evidence for the fact that he means creativity in a very broad sense, which includes the artist as a prototype of the higher type of man, but is not restricted to him.

The new attitude that Nietzsche seeks for man is not knowing, but creating. It is exemplified in "The Three Metamorphoses of the Spirit" in *Thus Spoke Zarathustra,* where the spirit changes from a camel, the load-bearing spirit who says "you must," to the lion, the destroyer of old values who says, "I will," to the child who alone has the power to create something new. The key word *power,* in the sense of ability, of being able to do something links the creating child to the artist, the *Künstler* who has the art (ability) of carrying out what he wants to do. Without getting lost in an etymological swamp it might be mentioned that creativity, *creare*, is possibly related to the word for growth, *crescere*, and this would fit in nicely with Nietzsche's idea of power as self-increase, ability.

If the two basic alternatives that philosophers have come up with to explain the nature of the world process are mechanism and teleology—both of which Nietzsche rejects—then a third, less explored possibility offers itself in Nietzsche's world that goes back to Heraclitus' child playing counters in a game. "Time is a child moving counters in a game; the royal power is a child's" (Fragment 54).

The world is not mechanistic, not teleological, but a play of forces increasing and decreasing in the innocence of becoming where there is no order already present in things, but a multitude of free possibilities for creativity to work.

It is precisely the fact that there is no predetermined mechanistic or teleological order in the world that enables man to be *radically* creative, that is, to create something that was not there before. If the world were a world of deterministic mechanism, man would be the billiard ball plaything of measurable forces, he would be sheerely re-active at best. If the world were a world of teleology, man would again be the plaything of some master mentality (a "total sensorium" as Nietzsche calls it) who uses him to attain some end that lies "outside" the world. But one of Nietzsche's most fundamental insights is that, because the world is not prestructured in either of these ways, or in any other conceivable way, there is truly room for man to shape the world and, above all, himself. In creating, he is *affirming* the world by transforming it. Nietzsche was right when he said that there is no such thing as a pessimistic or nihilistic artist. Art *is* affirmation.

To oversimplify the relation of creativity and decadence for purposes of clarity, we can say in conclusion that they are diametrically opposed in the way that Nietzsche conceives them. *Decadence* is the name for the present historical situation (a situation that has hardly changed since the time when Nietzsche was writing, but has rather become ominously intensified in a way perhaps unforseeable for him), a situation stifled by the "values" of morality, religion, and philosophy. Decadence is the powerless state of reacting to everything that ends in the feeling of *ressentiment* and the spirit of revenge against life. Creativity is the overcoming of this state, the ability to transform self and the world, and in this transformation to affirm what is as "baptized in the well of eternity and beyond good and evil" (*Thus Spoke Zarathustra* III, "Before Sunrise").

Those overpowering artists who let a *harmony* sound forth from every conflict are those who bestow upon things their own power and self-redemption: they express their innermost experience in the symbolism of every work of art they produce—their creativity is gratitude for their existence." (*The Will to Power*, No. 852)

CHAPTER THREE

Life Without Music

In a letter to Peter Gast dated January 15, 1888, Nietzsche wrote: "Life without music is simply an error, a strain, an exile."[1] This is one of the strongest of many testimonies to the absolutely central role of music in Nietzsche's life and thought. If Nietzsche regarded art as "the great stimulus to life," it was in music that he found the highest instance of that stimulus. Thus, it is perhaps precisely his criticism of a musician that can help throw some additional light on his thought. That musician is, of course, Richard Wagner.

Parenthetically, we might note that the attitude of most philosophers to the art of music has been, to say the least, shocking, not to say appalling. Brief quotations from two revered philosophers might serve to document this. The first is from Kant, the second from Hegel.

Besides, there attaches to music a certain want of urbanity from the fact that, chiefly from the character of its instruments, it extends its influence further than is desired (in the neighborhood), and so as it were obtrudes itself and does violence to the freedom of others who are not of the musical company. The arts which appeal to the eyes do not do this, for we need only turn our eyes away if we

27

wish to avoid being impressed. The case of music is almost like that of the delight derived from a smell that diffuses itself widely. The man who pulls his perfumed handkerchief out of his pocket attracts the attention of all around him, even against their will, and he forces them, if they are to breathe at all, to enjoy the scent; hence this habit has gone out of fashion.[2]

Music, for example, which has exclusively to deal with the entirely undefined motion of the soul within, with the musical tones of that which is, relatively, feeling denuded of positive thought, has little or no need to bring home to consciousness the substance of intellectual conception. For this very reason musical talent declares itself as a rule in very early youth, when the head is still empty and the emotions have barely had a flutter; it has, in fact, attained real distinction at a time in the artist's life when both intelligence and life are practically without experience. And for the matter of that we often enough see very great accomplishment in musical composition and execution hung together with considerable indigence of mind and character.[3]

However, to go to the other extreme like Schopenhauer and exalt music straight out of sight is not much help either. It is difficult for most of us to see how "music gives the *universalia ante rem*," how it embodies the Will.

It is well known that Nietzsche gave a great deal of thought to "the case of Wagner": explicitly, *The Birth of Tragedy,* which was dedicated to Wagner; the essay, "Richard Wagner in Bayreuth"; *The Case of Wagner, Nietzsche Contra Wagner* (composed of excerpts from earlier works), as well as countless passages and remarks from virtually all his writings, including the *Nachlass.*

Thus, it might be well worth our while to take a fresh look at why Nietzsche was bothered, musically and philosophically, by Richard Wagner.

Most philosophers opt for one or the other side of the balancing scale between rationalism and irrationalism insofar as they consider both sides seriously at all. Nietzsche saw in rationalism *and* irrationalism two major dangers to the development of philosophy and culture in general.

Rationalism

The roots of Nietzsche's critique of rationalism go back to *The Birth of Tragedy*, that chaotically brilliant and visionary work of the 24 year old. The two culprits whom he indicts here are Euripides and Socrates: Euripides, because he brought the spectator (consciousness) on stage who thus usurped the living, Dionysian reality of the chorus; Socrates, because he was a first sign of decadence in that he placed reason above instinct and in opposition to it. In Socrates, Nietzsche sees the beginning of the history of the supremacy of reason at the expense of what he calls *instinct, feeling, the senses,* and so forth, in short, the whole group of man's faculties that has indeed been more or less denigrated by Western philosophy until the postIdealists in the nineteenth century. It is these factulties that he looks to as antinihilistic and creative. In *Ecce Homo* Nietzsche states that already in *The Birth of Tragedy* he recognized "'Reason' at any rate as a dangerous, life-undermining force."[4]

At this stage Nietzsche is not worried about the opposite problem, irrationalism yet, a problem that has subsequently received less *philosophic* attention than his critique of rationalism. This chapter will concentrate on Nietzsche's treatment of the problem of irrationalism insofar as it is instantiated by Wagner. We are interested not so much in the question of whether Nietzsche is "right" about Wagner, as in catching sight of the phenomenon that he is characterizing. Drawing a certain parallel, we could say that what Nietzsche caught in his critique of Socrates (and Plato) as rationalists was not an exhaustively accurate characterization of those thinkers but rather the "ism" growing out of them, an "ism" that had tremendous historical consequences as he himself forsaw.

In some ways it is easier to see what Nietzsche is getting at under the title of *irrationalism* in his writings on Schopenhauer. But even if that might be easier, it is perhaps more concretely illuminating to see, to *"hear,"* as it were, that phenomenon in Wagner, more subtle, more audible, more insidiously seductive.

Irrationalism

Turning now to Nietzsche's critique of irrationalism, we wish to discuss three things: (1) the concrete criticism of Wagner, (2) the philosphical meaning of that criticism, and (3) what alternative possibility of "creativity" Nietzsche envisaged because creativity is, after all, a major theme in his work.

Concrete Criticism of Wagner

As self-contradictory as Nietzsche can often appear on the surface, he is remarkably self-consistent when it

comes to talking about Wagner. There is no uncertainty
and no wavering here. Briefly stated, Nietzsche sees in
Wagner the actor who subordinates music to the rank of
a mere means. Wagner does not communicate, he hyp-
notizes.

How the soul is supposed to move according to the new
music. The artistic intention which the new music pursues
in what is now called, forcefully but unclearly, "infinite
melody," can be clarified by going into the ocean, gradually losing our sure step on the bottom and finally giving
ourselves over to that surging element for better or for
worse: one should *swim.* In previous older music one was
supposed to *dance* in a delicate or ceremonious or fiery
back and forth, faster or slower: the necessary measure,
keeping certain equally balanced degrees of time and
energy demanded of the listener's soul a continuous
reflective awareness. . . . Richard Wagner wanted another
kind of *movement of the soul* which, as we said, is related
to swimming and floating. Perhaps this is the most essential of his innovations. His most famous means, originat-
ing from this will and adapted to it—"infinite melody"
strives to break every mathematical regularity in time and
energy, even to mock; and it is overly rich in inventing
those effects which sound like rhythmic paradoxes and
vicious speeches to the older ear. It is afraid of becoming
stone, of crystallization, of music's transition to the archi-
tectonic. . . . From conveniently imitating such art a great
danger can arise for music. Next to an overripeness of
rhythmic feeling there has always lurked in hiding a kind
of growing wild, a disintegration of rhythm. This danger
becomes very great when such music depends more and
more closely on a completely naturalistic art of acting
and a language of gesture that are not educated and ruled

by any higher plastic form, an art and a language that have
no measure in themselves and are unable to communicate
any measure to the element nestling in them, the *all too
feminine* essence of music.[5]

This music takes our feet off the ground. We are no
longer able to *dance* (and Nietzsche's Zarathustra had
said that he would only believe in a god who could
dance), we can only swirl and float along with infinite
melody, a tortuous, sinuous striving that evades any res-
olution, punctuation, or caesura. Nietzsche discovered
in Wagner an auditory version of Hegel's "bad infinite."

Musically speaking, what Nietzsche objected to in Wagner was this infinite melody coupled with a heavy dose of
chromaticism, and lacking a defined sense of intrinsic
rhythm.[6] He also objected to the elements of realism bordering on imitation. The music became too "explicit."

Basically, Nietzsche's criticism amounts to saying that-
Wagner subordinated music to his theatrical purposes,
that he degraded music to a mere means and tried to force
it to perform ideological functions which are totally alien
to it. Music is at once too concrete and too abstract to be
effectively specific. Its concreteness resides in the sound
itself, its abstractness resides in the fact that it *represents*
nothing, it has no object. In a less technical way, Nietzsche is taking the same position as his contemporary, the
gifted musical critic, Eduard Hanslick.

Above all, Wagner represents the actor, a type who is
subjected to considerable derision in *Thus Spoke Zarathustra*.

You do not know who Wagner is; a first-rate actor. . . .
The actor Wagner is a tyrant; his pathos topples every

taste, every resistance. Who equals the persuasive power of these gestures?—Who else envisages gestures with such assurance, so clearly from the start? The way Wagner's pathos holds its breath, refuses to let go an extreme feeling, achieves a terrifying *duration* of states when even a moment threatens to strangle us—

Was Wagner a musician at all? At any rate, there was something else that he was more: Namely, an incomparable histrio, the greatest mime, the most amazing genius of the theater ever among Germans, our *scenic artist par excellence*. He belongs elsewhere, not in the history of music. As a musician, too, he was only what he was in general, he *became* a musician, he *became* a poet because the tyrant within him, his actor's genius, compelled him. One cannot begin to figure out Wanger until one figures out his dominant instinct.

Wagner was *not* a musician by instinct. He showed this by abandoning all lawfulness and, more precisely, all style in music in order to turn it into what he required, theatrical rhetoric, a means of expression, of underscoring gestures, of suggestion, of the psychologically picturesque.[7]

Nietzsche acknowledges Wagner as a genius of the stage, of gesture, as a first-rate actor. We are fascinated, even hypnotized, by the awesomeness taking place on the stage, by the Norse metaphysics of gods, dragons, giants, dwarfs. The human, at-all-human element is missing. This was not at all Nietzsche's vision of the more than human-all-too-human. It was simply not-human.

As a matter of fact, he repeated a single proposition all his life long: that his music did not mean mere music. But more. But infinitely more. —"Not *mere* music"—no musician would say that. . . . "Music is always a mere means": that was his theory, that above all the only *practice* open to him. But no musician would think that way.[8]

To sum up the concrete criticism, Wagner was the arch target for Nietzsche's attack on the romantic, the decadent, on a kind of glorification of feeling stemming from hunger and a lack, as opposed to superabundance and power.

Philosophical Meaning of Nietzsche's Criticism

This last remark leads us straight into the issue of what Nietzsche was attacking philosophically as well as musically. Of course, this is not some new, separate, isolated factor, but forms the very core of his whole philosophy. The case of Wagner is not some offshoot of Nietzsche's general inquiry, but instantiates with an almost pathological sensitivity the gist of his whole crusade against the romanticism of great passion.[9] It is not all feeling that he rejects, but a kind of feeling that betrays a peculiar mixture of *ressentiment*, powerlessness, and wishfulness; in short, a kind of feeling that is evidence of a weakness that would make demands.

> Romanticism: an ambiguous question, like everything
> modern.
> The aesthetic states twofold.
> The full and bestowing as opposed to the seeking,
> desiring.[10]

Ultimately for Nietzsche it is a question of *motive*, not only and never primarily in the psychological sense, but in the sense of what *moves* us to do something, to do anything.

"Is art a consequence of *dissatisfaction with reality?* Or an expression of *gratitude for happiness* enjoyed? In the former case, *romanticism;* in the latter, aureole, dithyramb (in short, art of apotheosis)."[11]

Perhaps the most comprehensive formulation of Nietzsche's position lies in the following fragment:

> *What is romanticism?*—In regard to all aesthetic values, I now employ this fundamental distinction: I ask in each individual case "has hunger or superabundance become creative here?" At first sight, another distinction might seem more plausible—it is far more obvious—namely the distinction whether the desire for rigidity, eternity, *"being"* has been the cause of creation, or rather the desire for destruction, for change, for *becoming.* But both kinds of desire prove, when examined more closely, to be ambiguous and interpretable according to the scheme mentioned above, which, I think, is to be preferred.
>
> The desire for destruction, change, becoming, *can* be the expression of an overfull power pregnant with the future (my term for this, as is known, is the word "Dionysian"); but it can also be the hatred of the ill-constituted, disinherited, underprivileged, which destroys, *has* to destroy, because what exists, indeed existence itself, all being itself, enrages it and provokes it.
>
> "Eternalization," on the other hand, *can* proceed from gratitude and love—an art of this origin will always be an art of apotheosis, dithyrambic perhaps with Rubens, blissful with Hafiz, bright and gracious with Goethe, and shedding a Homeric aureole over all things—but it can also be that tyrannic will of a great sufferer who would like to forge what is most personal, individual, and narrow—most idiosyncratic—in his suffering, into a binding *law* and compulsion, taking revenge on all things, as it

were, by impressing, forcing and branding into them his image, the image of his torture. The latter is romantic pessimism in its most expressive form, whether as Schopenhauerian philosophy of will or as Wagnerian music.[12]

The types of higher men that Nietzsche portrays, particularly in *Thus Spoke Zarathustra*, center around the saint, the ascetic and the artist. All are men who have worked to overcome themselves with some measure of success, even if, as in the first two cases, they did this for reasons that have lost their validity. Given the *artist* as the highest type of human being Nietzsche was able to present to us, we find four inextricably related phenomena that have to do with the *classical* artist, the active, as opposed to the re-active, romantic artist. These four phenomena are beauty, the grand style, power, and God. Leaving aside the question of God as such, as lying outside the scope of this chapter, let us examine what Nietzsche sought as the antithesis of romanticism, often loosely associated under the general term *classical*. But we must bear in mind that what the romantics in Germany protested against was not classicism, but rather reason, enlightenment, taste, the eighteenth century.[13] Nietzsche is dealing with the terms *classic* and *romantic* not so much as historical periods, but rather as principles of style perhaps best exemplified by, but not restricted to, any specific historical period.

"Beauty" is for the artist something outside all orders of rank, because in beauty opposites are tamed; the highest sign of power, namely, power over opposites; moreover, without tension: —that violence is no longer needed; that

everything follows, obeys, so easily and so pleasantly—
That is what delights the artist's will to power.[14]

Beauty, power, and the grand style all have to do with
the taming of or mastery over opposites, with gathering
them into a higher dynamic unity. Nietzsche then expresses the concern that, of all the arts, music alone has
failed to achieve this style and voices his fear that the grand
style might be incompatible with the very nature of music.

All the arts know such aspirants to the grand style: why
are they lacking in music? No musician has yet built as
that architect did who created the Palazzo Pitti—Here
lies a problem. Does music perhaps belong to that culture
in which the domain of men of force of all kinds has
ceased? Does the concept grand style ultimately stand in
contradiction to the soul of music—to the "woman" in
our music?—

I here touch upon a cardinal question: where does our
entire music belong? The ages of classical taste knew
nothing to compare with it: it began to blossom when the
Renaissance world had attained its evening, when "freedom" had departed from morals and even from men:—is
it part of its character to be counter-Renaissance? Is it the
sister of the Baroque style, since it is in any case its contemporary? Is music, modern music, not already decadence?

Once before I pointed to this question: whether our
music is not a piece of counter-Renaissance in art?
whether it is not next-of-kin to the Baroque style?
whether it has not grown up in contradiction to all classical taste, so that all ambitions to become classical are forbidden to it by its nature?[15]

Creativity

What is the "solution" proposed by Nietzsche to this predicament? How can art in general and music in particular achieve the grand style? Does Nietzsche ever tell us more concretely what the grand style is and does he manage to define creativity in a way that goes beyond sentimental banalities?

We might best proceed with these questions by citing one of Nietzsche's favorite opponents, Hegel.

> In all respects art is and remains for us, on the side of its highest possibilities, a thing of the past. Herein it has further lost its genuine truth and life, and is rather transported to our world of *ideas* that is able to maintain its former necessity and its superior place in reality. What is now stimulated in us by works of art is, in addition to the fact of immediate enjoyment, our judgment. A *science* of art is therefore a far more urgent necessity in our own days than in times when art as art sufficed by itself alone to give complete satisfaction. We are invited by art to contemplate it reflectively, not, that is to say, with the object of recreating such art, but in order to ascertain scientifically its nature.[16]

Hegel felt that art was no longer capable of adequately expressing the highest truths. The "content" of Absolute Spirit had simply outgrown the "form" of art, Absolute Spirit cannot fittingly be portrayed in visual form. Nietzsche reverses Hegel. He does not do this intentionally because we have no evidence that he ever concerned himself with Hegel's philosophy of art. Rather, Nietzsche's initial artistic vision of *The Birth of Tragedy* grows into the deepening insight that knowledge is not

going to provide an "answer" to the question of life. Far
from saying with Hegel that art is no longer adequate to
express the "truth" (of Absolute Spirit), Nietzsche abandons the whole idea of truth as something essential to
human life. The problem of truth in Nietzsche is far too
complex to go into here, but we can safely extrapolate
the basic tenets that "art is the truly metaphysical activity of life," that "art is *worth more* than truth," and that
"art is the great stimulus to life." On the whole, Nietzsche does not believe it is possible to know truth objectively in a fluctuating world of the will to power, and
even if it were, it simply is not his major concern. Nietzsche is passionately interested, not in truth, but in
meaning. And, as the theologian Paul Tillich, citing
Nietzsche, pointed out, the threat of our present time is
precisely meaninglessness.

The world that Nietzsche shows us can be either a terrifying or a liberating experience. Nietzsche himself was
keenly aware of this and often commented that it was a
matter of strength in the question of how much truth,
how much illness or adversity one could endure. What
was frightening to one individual might act as a stimulus
to another. Thus faced with Nietzsche's pronouncement
of the death of God and with his doctrine of eternal
recurrence, one might very well decide that the world is
meaningless, without purpose or sense. This would be
the type of person who expects reality to be, so to speak,
pregiven and prestructured. The artist would have no
such feeling of terror or futility or even disappointment,
but would welcome the challenge of shaping and struc-
turing the world himself. He would be radically free.
Thus, perhaps the closest Nietzsche ever came to giving

us a foretoken of the *Übermensch* was in the artist-philosopher, whereby the component philosopher must not be understood in the academic sense, but as a thinker in Nietzsche's vein of *Redlichkeit* (honesty, openness). "The *artist*-philosopher. Higher concept of art. Whether a man can place himself so far distant from other men that he can form them? (Preliminary exercises: (1) he who forms himself, the hermit; (2) the artist hitherto, as a perfecter on a small scale, working on material."[17]

It turns out that we can look to Nietzsche only for general intimations about creativity and the grand style, not for anything specifically musical. In turning away from Wagner, Nietzsche seemed to search in inappropriate fields for a kind of replacement, in composers such as Bizet, Offenbach, and of course, his devoted friend and disciple, Peter Gast, about whom we can safely assume from the silence of history that we have not missed out on too much.

We close these fragmentary musings with a quote that points to what Nietzsche experienced, but never quite managed to communicate fully: "Far above Wagner I have seen music in tragedy. Far above Schopenhauer I have heard the music in the tragedy of existence."[18]

CHAPTER FOUR

Thoughts on Pity and Revenge

Pity and the spirit of revenge are two fundamental
human attitudes portrayed in Nietzsche's thought. At
first glance, one might wonder why just these two attitudes would be significant for him, and in what possible
context. This chapter will attempt to examine the two
attitudes with regard to their psychological significance
for the individual and with regard to their universal or
ontological significance, that is, for Nietzsche, with
regard to their implications for the nature of life itself. I
purposely call them *attitudes*, for they are not mere, subjective emotions or feelings. They are attitudes in the
sense of a stance, a position with regard to life. It is these
attitudes as such that I wish to explore, and not their significance in Nietzsche's thought alone.In other words, I
am using Nietzsche as a kind of springboard to gain
access to the meaning of these two attitutdes in general.

The words *psychological* or individual and *ontological*
or universal are not very adequate, but they can function
as makeshift terms. *Psychological* refers to individual,
specific instances alone, whereas *ontological* refers to a
more or less permanent attitude of universal significance,
somewhat akin to Aristotle's definition of metaphysics

as describing generic traits of being. Nietzsche, as he himself remarked, "liked to sit on many different rungs of his ladder," and his spheres of analysis range from what is fairly familiar to what is profoundly thought.

Most, if not all, of the basic concepts in Nietzsche's writings are concerned with precisely the question of a stance toward life. This is perhaps most evident in his proclamation of the death of God, more generally expressed, the loss of any kind of transcendence whatever. At least three other basic themes are related to the proclamation of the death of God, and thus to the question of a stance toward life: the overman, transvaluation of all values and the less known concept of "the innocence of becoming." If God is dead, the question arises as to who shall give meaning to the earth, and Nietzsche's search for the answer to this question leads him to the problematic and often misunderstood concept of the overman. It is the overman who is supposed to effect a transvaluation of all values, to give value to the earth itself and cease placing all value in a transcendent world that does not exist, thereby losing everything in self-deception. Finally, the phrase *innocence of becoming* means that the world of becoming, *our* world is no longer to be judged and condemned as an imperfect copy of the world of being, but rather to be affirmed just as it is. Individual existence is not hybris, not a crime against nature, as the Greeks presumably thought it was, it is innocent.

To return to the concepts of pity and revenge, I shall distinguish three different concepts of pity and two of revenge. This is admittedly rather complicated, but I believe it is warranted. Pity includes (1) individual psy-

chological pity explicit in Nietzsche, (2) universal, ontological pity implicit in Nietzsche, and (3) compassion,
not in Nietzsche at all. Revenge includes (1) individual
psychological revenge explicit in Nietzsche, and (2) universal ontological revenge implicit in Nietzsche. I should
like to state preliminarily that Nietzsche has two distinct
concepts of pity, which he fails to distinguish from each
other. One concept is the most explicit, and incorporates
the idea that to pity someone is to place oneself above
him, to look down upon his unfortunate state and feel
sorry for him, not without a sense of self-elevation. This
would reflect the individual concept of pity in that it is
restricted to a certain situation with no further-reaching
implications for the nature of life or humanity in general.
This kind of pity lies very close to what Nietzsche calls
ressentiment or a psychological form of revenge. In fact,
the core of this chapter will consist in showing that individual psychological pity and individual psychological
revenge are fundamentally identical and that ontological
compassion and ontological revenge are dead opposites.

Because pity and revenge as psychological attitudes
are familiar to us all, I shall spend less time on them.
Everyone knows what it means to have pity for someone
in a certain situation, be it as true compassion or in Nietzsche's more limited understanding of pity as self-elevation. Pity and revenge become really interesting when
they are attitudes not related to an individual, but to the
whole of life.

I have the spirit of revenge against someone who has
somehow harmed me. The motive of my revenge is to
restore what I have lost or suffered by "getting back" at
the person who harmed me.On the overt level, an exam-

ple of this would be an old-fashioned duel at dawn for the sake of challenged honor or the shooting of an unfaithful lover. The most subtle level of revenge might lie in what Nietzsche calls *ressentiment*, which appears to be more a general state or feeling, whereas revenge implies at least the possibility of some active retaliation. *Ressentiment* or resentment is frequently an attitude that is not even expressed in words and may not even be recognized by the person who has it.

Pity in the sense of self-elevation is simply another way of retaliation, in the form of lowering and debasing another person. The person has not succeeded, did not gain acknowledgment, and so forth, and I, who supposedly have gained some measure of success—but not enough—can compete with him to my advantage. This kind of pity—which probably is not so widespread as Nietzsche thought it was—is sheerly competitive. Had the person succeeded, he would have been a potential threat to me. In pitying him I take revenge for the very possibility that he might have succeeded or might still succeed at some future time. Pity turns out to be nothing but a form of revenge.

To turn now to pity and revenge on a universal level, let us consider Nietzsche's statement about the death of God.

Nietzsche makes two seemingly different statements about *how* the death of God came about, and each incorporates one of the two concepts of pity and revenge. Before examining these statements, a few words must be said about what Nietzsche understands by *God*. God is primarily the God of Christianity, particularly of Christian morality. Christianity, says Nietzsche, is Platonism for the people. Thus the death of God means the death of the realm of Platonic Ideas as Nietzsche conceived them, the death of any possible realm transcending man. Man has lost the meaningful center in terms of which he can understand his existence and his finitude. The loss of this center leads Nietzsche to ask for something in terms of which man can understand himself as something other and more than just, for example, "the sum of his actions" (Sartre).

To return to Nietzsche's statements on how the death of God came about, Nietzsche states that "God, too, has his hell: it is his love for man. God is dead, God died of his pity for man."

I should like to exclude the meaning of pity as self-elevation from now on, because it no longer makes sense in this context. What Nietzsche means here is pity in the sense of really "feeling sorry for" and I shall retain the word *pity* with that meaning. Then I should like to make a further distinction that Nietzsche could not make linguistically, but also did not make in terms of meaning, a distinction between pity and compassion. There is only one word in German for both of these phenomena: *Mitleid*. *Mitleid* is etymologically equivalent to compassion, but in actual usage is closer to pity. I shall discuss pity in terms of feeling sorry for and then try at the end of this chapter to inquire into compassion as distinct from any kind of pity in Nietzsche's sense of that word.

The other statement or statements about how the death of God came about asserts that man killed God out of the spirit of revenge. Because this is perhaps the more problematic of the two assertions, I shall start by discussing pity.

If God dies of his pity for man, pity would indeed have to be a very powerful, deadly force. This would appear to contradict the ordinary idea of pity as a passive, commiserating attitude. To pity someone is to feel sorry for him. Obviously this cannot exhaust what Nietzsche means by pity when he speaks of it as the greatest sin, the greatest temptation.

Nietzsche's interest in the phenomenon of pity grew out of his early preoccupation with Schopenhauer, but it did not remain within the confines of Schopenhauer's thought. Schopenhauer adopted the Buddhist idea of compassion in his philosophy, stating that one should have compassion for one's fellow living beings because individuality is fundamentally an illusion. We are all basically nothing but the One Will to Live, this needy, struggling, insatiable Will, biting its teeth into its own flesh, producing this "worst of all possible worlds." The nature of the Will, and therefore of the world, is suffering. Given this sorry state of affairs, we all need compassion for each other, and we are all fundamentally identical anyhow.

Nietzsche starts out polemically by rejecting the desirability of pitying one's fellow man. On a metaphysical level, he neither believes that the nature of the world is suffering nor does he believe in Schopenhauer's metaphysical Primal Unity, the Will to Live, which guarantees a somewhat disastrous identity of all beings. On a certain level of experience, most of what Nietzsche says about pity makes very good sense and would probably be acceptable to most of us. Let us say that I have a good friend who is badly injured in an automobile accident. The friend has to adjust to his new life situation, for example, restricted use of his arm with prognosis for some improvement. When I am with that friend, I do him no favor by telling him how sorry I am for him and what a terrible, unjust thing has befallen him. In pitying him, the crucial issue is not that of degrading him and raising myself to a superior position, as Nietzsche would say. The crucial danger is that I might equate his whole being with that state of misfortune. Pity in the sense of feeling sorry for seems to exclude all else of significance, it simply engulfs the man pitied and paralyzes him.

If I refrain from pitying my friend in a particular situation, such as the automobile accident, I do it for his sake and for no one else's. But if nothing particularly disastrous has happened to a friend and yet I feel pity for him because he is somehow miserable or depressed for no palpable reason, the issue becomes more ominous. To have pity for someone in the sense distiniguished here could mean that his whole being, not just his present situation, is pitiable, even piteous or wretched. From here it is but a short step to the question not only of my friend's total life situation, but of everyone's situation, of life itself. In this sense, to have pity would mean to acknowledge and acquiesce in human suffering, in fact, to admit that the human condition is one of suffering. To make a point analogous to Nietzsche's distinction between a passive nihilism of despair and an active nihilism searching for honest affirmation, one could say here that the only possible antidote to passive pity would be the active pity described but not named as such in *Thus Spoke Zarathustra* as "passing by." *Passing by* means that when there is absolutely nothing that you can do for someone in his present situation, you grit your teeth and walk on. You leave him alone. Otherwise pity can very easily turn into worry, which I would describe as a state of agitation frantically or less frantically searching for "what to do," but essentially incapable of action. The etymological root of worry is to strangle (as in the German *Würgen*). The worrier, which we probably all are to some extent, tends to "strangle" both himself and the person about whom he is worrying.

The extreme outcome of passive pity as acquiescence in human suffering lies in what Nietzsche calls *disgust* or nausea with regard to life in general. When the worrier ceases to "care," he lands in disgust. The implication is that to acknowledge totally that someone is truly and completely in a state of suffering, myself or anyone else, means to acknowledge that state of suffering to be the ultimate human condition. Nietzsche's formulation of this acknowledgement is, "Nothing matters, nothing is worthwhile, knowledge strangles." I believe what Nietzsche is saying is that if we are ever brought to admit the ultimacy of this state, we shall never get out of it. The implication is that an attitude of genuine, affirmative compassion, as distinct from any sense of pity, can come only from someone who knows that suffering is not the ultimate reality. Otherwise that attitude is one of pity. I realize that this sounds paradoxical in that the attitude of pity presumably assumes a superior position (*I* am OK; you are not, poor devil) and that the attitude of compassion would seem to come from someone perhaps "in the same boat." But I should still like to retain a sense of compassion that is more ultimate, more all-embracing, and more affirmative than pity. The compassion stemming from a true affirmation of life would be able to affirm even the most terrible suffering, not just commiserate with it. A true life affirmation would have to be able to affirm *all* of life, not just its more pleasant moments. This is admittedly an extremely difficult point of view to attain, if not impossible for most of us. Nietzsche vacillates in his thinking between the two extreme possibilities of nihilism and affirmation. He often reached an affirmative point of view in terms of his own experience, but he was never able to see that affirmation as a concrete reality for mankind as a whole. Affirmation remained for him at best a possibility intensely sought, but subject to the question of man's strength and abilities. This was his whole question with regard to his doctrine of eternal recurrence. If one could wish to live his life over and over again, exactly as it is with its sufferings and its joys, this would be a true affirmation of life. This would be a kind of "existential" life affirmation, a willingness or even the desire to live through everything again as opposed to, for example, Leibniz's logically derived statement that this is the best of all possible worlds. But to be able to do this, one would have to free oneself from the spirit of revenge, to which I now turn. In other words, the spirit of revenge precludes any possible sense of compassion as an affirmative attitude, which I still have to develop.

The spirit of revenge seems to be a less universal phenomenon than pity. It would appear to crop up in isolated, extreme situations, not to be applicable to the human situation as such, as might well be pity. Pity is pervasive, revenge is not. I might quite easily and quite frequently have pity for anything I run accross, a dead chipmunk on the highway, a blind man begging, an ill child, a terribly old man struggling out to get his daily groceries. The spirit of revenge, on the other hand, occurs less frequently. I need to be involved in a long, intolerable situation before I am provoked into the spirit of revenge. And when that finally happens, I need a lot of time and wits to plot and accomplish my revenge effectively.

But Nietzsche really takes revenge as an ontological concept, a concept pervading all experience. First of all we have the statement that man killed God out of the spirit of revenge. He took revenge on God because God was an eternal witness, ever watching and pitying him.

> "But he *had* to die: he saw with eyes that saw everything;
> he saw man's depth and ultimate grounds, all his con-
> cealed disgrace and ugliness. His pity knew no shame: he
> crawled into my dirtiest nooks. This most curious, over-
> obtrusive, overpitying one had to die. He always saw me:
> on such a witness I wanted to have revenge or not live
> myself. The god who saw everything, *even man*—this
> god had to die! Man cannot bear it if such a witness
> should live."

This "god" is the epitome of the opposite of the attitude of passing by. He has created man as an independent being and now dwells in the attitude of observing
the suffering of his creation. He cannot pass by man in
his present state, he must watch, fascinated by a kind of
voyeuristic curiosity, the kind of curiosity that one can
often observe in a crowd standing around a bad automobile accident. God's pity has the effect of paralyzing
man—there is a parallel here to Sartre's *le regard*, the
look—who becomes incapable of action. *"Even man,"*
Nietzsche emphasizes, and should well have said *precisely* man. For man is the animal who *knows* he is being

observed and pitied. To act and reach a new dimension in which he can absolutely affirm life, man must kill god.

This action stemming from the spirit of revenge is the highest thing of which the spirit of revenge is capable. It corresponds in some ways to the lion in Nietzsche's three Metamorphoses of the Spirit. But Nietzsche feels that we have hitherto never gotten beyond the spirit of revenge, the lion. However, the analogy of the spirit of revenge with the lion has its limitations, even its dangers. Unlike the lion, the spirit of revenge is exclusively retaliative and harbors within itself the fatal trend of getting caught in abject dependency upon its object. It always remains re-action, it is never action.

But what happens when the spirit of revenge is not related to other human beings as some form of retaliation (*ressentiment*), but rather to life itself? This is perhaps the level of Nietzsche's most profound insight into the spirit of revenge. That insight is no longer concerned with the question of "getting back at" a person, but with the question of a furiously impotent denial of life. Nietzsche's astonishing contention is that all of man's best thinking until now has arisen from such an attitude of life denial. He would not say with Schopenhauer that we ought to deny the will to live. That would be pessimism. He is rather saying that there is a tremendous possibility for affirming life, but that no one has ever been able to do this except under the guise of a projection of some metaphysical, transcendent reality, a projection that can ultimately be traced back to the spirit of revenge. The spirit of revenge reasons as follows: This world, this life lacks meaning; therefore another, better world *must* exist above and beyond this one. The meaning of life *cannot* lie in the here and now, it *must* lie in some afterlife or God or other world. Thus the spirit of revenge takes revenge on the here and now; that is, kills it.

The most extensive analysis of the spirit of revenge is to be found in the section of *Thus Spoke Zarathustra* entitled "Redemption." What Nietzsche means by redemption or release lies in the relation of the will to time. This relation has until now always been characterized by—the spirit of revenge.

> "It was"—That is the name of the will's gnashing of teeth and most secret melancholy. Powerless against what has been done, he is an angry spectator of all that is past. This will cannot will backwards; and that he cannot break time and time's covetousness, that is the will's loneliest melancholy. . . . That time does not run backwards, that is his wrath; . . . and on all who can suffer he wreaks revenge for his inability to go backwards. This, indeed, this alone, is what *revenge* is: the will's ill-will against time and its "it was."

Revenge is the will's ill-will against time and its "it was." The will as ill-will is the antithesis of the Will to Power; it is powerless against what has been done. The will as ill-will cannot go backward; it cannot break time and time's desire. The ill-will is precisely the will that wills, that *must* will against the irreversibility of time.

The will that is the Will to Power must will something far higher than reconciliation with time. Nietzsche asks, How does this come about? Who taught the will to will backward?

The redemption of the past comes about when every "it was" is transformed into "thus I willed it." Does this mean that the will is confronted with the "it was" as something irrevocable and inalterable, something it can no longer do anything about, and then says to itself: That is exactly what I willed? Is this retroactive affirmation not a kind of desperate heroism of the will? Can it really redeem the past? Would it not, on the contrary, defeat itself, give up in a fury of impotence and renounce all willing? And how could all of this reverse time?

The will that is the Will to Power does not simply say: "Thus I willed it." It also says: "Thus do I will it, thus shall I will it!" The *whole* of time is here at stake. The past that is to be redeemed somehow contains time as a whole within itself. But time as a whole is eternal return.

The most obvious interpretation of reconciliation with time as a whole would be that the past is affirmed, and then its endless repetition, its coming again and again, is also affirmed. However, this interpretation equates the "it was" with some past event and approaches what Nietzsche calls *Turkish fatalism*, when man stands before the future with folded hands. The "it was" is not something that was once there is the past and is now causing the will to stumble if it wants to will forward. The "it was" is a fragment, so to speak, a piece of crystallized, rigidified time until the creating will says to it: "But thus I willed it!"

One must consider Nietzsche's exact mode of expression here. He does not speak of redemption from *time*, but rather of redemption from *revenge*. What is related to time is not redemption, not even reconciliation. "The will which is the Will to Power must will something far higher than reconciliation."

Revenge is the will's ill-will against time and its "it was."Revenge seeks for what is responsible, for what has robbed, existence of its innocence. Redemption from revenge consists in winning back the "innocence of becoming."

The instinct of revenge looks for a ground, a reason for its suffering, *suffering* in the broadest sense of undergoing something. *Suffering* in this sense is an "ontological" concept, not a pessimistic one governed by wishful thinking (I suffer, the world is "bad" (*pessimus*), I wish it were otherwise, it ought to be otherwise); for the Will to Power is not Being, not Becoming, but a Pathos. This cause or reason can lie only in the past, in the "it was." The "it was" thus becomes the cause for the present, which, however, then loses its true character of presence and becomes a mere consequence, a powerless continuance of the past. The present is thus irrevocably lost before it can even begin to be, because as a consequence (effect) it can never get behind its cause which must always be "before" it. Given this meaning of the irreversibility of time, it is absolutely impossible for the will to will backward. The meaning of the "it was," of the past in general, lies not in losing the present through its flowing by into the past. Rather, the "it was" obstructs every possibility of the occurrence of any real present. The meaning of finitude implicit here is not that everything passes away, but that everything is rigidified in the past, more exactly that everything has always become rigidified because of the unconditioned, inexorable priority of the inaccessible, past cause. Thus eternal return is truly meaningless, because it occurs on the temporal foundation of the "it was," of the "always-already-there." Recurrence is not only a superfluous repetition, it is nihilistic; that is, any possible originality of occurring, anything new whatsoever, is annihilated by the foundation of the "it was." The here and now referred to earlier is killed before it can even begin to be.

Zarathustra understands himself as the advocate and justifier of all finitude. If this world is not the pale, imperfect copy of a world of Platonic ideas or any other kind of transcendent realm, existence cannot be thought of as "eternally recurring deed and guilt" measured against that realm. With this doctrine of eternal return, Nietzsche attempted a "reconcilation" of the will with time by affirming existence just as it is, and then going on to transform it.

I do not wish to go into Nietzsche's highly problematic doctrine of eternal return here or even raise the question to what extent it actually succeeds in offering a possibility of affirming life.[1] By way of concluding, I should like to concentrate on the question of life affirmation that is incompatible with the attitudes of pity and revenge and that is the only possible basis for compassion, in the nonsentimental sense of "sympathy" or even empathy.

If I cannot affirm existence just as it is, any attempt to transform it falls back into the negatively oriented spirit of revenge that can do nothing. But if I am able to affirm existence as it is, then I gain freedom, the freedom that Nietzsche calls "the splendid 'I can' of the artist." If I can affirm out of the fullness of my existence instead of revenging myself for what I lack or have lost or could lose, I am freed from the bonds of reaction and gain a new dimension of freedom.

Paradoxically, it is only when I can affirm existence just as it is that I become free to transform it. As Nietzsche says in the *Will to Power*, "man becomes the transfigurer of existence when he learns to transfigure himself." This transformation is something that no god can give or impose on any man nor, for that matter, any human being on another.

When Nietzsche says that art is of more value than truth, he does not mean that we should all flee from some terrible "truth" into a world of fantasy. There is no fixed, hard and fast "truth." It simply does not exist in the sense of the traditional correspondence theory of an idea with its object or even in the sense of any fixed given "reality." The artist is the man who shapes his own life experience, not just statues or string quartets, and thus truly *is*, instead of staring helplessly at so-called reality and lamenting his supposed fate.

Nietzsche's strong emphasis on the question of affirmation and being active in contradistinction to nihilism and being passive seems at first to be a kind of ethical side issue, or at worst an overwrought glorification of a dubious optimism. But this is not so. It is perhaps the most fundamental issue in his thinking because it *undercuts* any other kind of distinction. It is not so important whether I am Apollonian or Dionysian, classic or romantic, whether I believe in being or in becoming. What is crucial is precisely the attitude or stance from which I believe in the Apollonian or the Dionysian, in being or becoming, an attitude that, if it is genuine, first authenticates, bears witness to, and grounds what is believed in. This attitude is not "subjective" for the simple reason that Nietzsche does not believe in the "subject." Man, the still undetermined animal, takes up a stance that becomes his center of experience, his attitude from which he shapes experience.

It is only from an affirmative attitude freed from the spirit of revenge that something like compassion becomes possible. If I can affirm life, I will never equate a particular situation of misfortune or suffering with life itself. But the question remains: How can I affirm precisely that situation of suffering just as it is if I do not wish to treat it as philosophers have treated the problem of evil, by saying that evil is really just a lack of good, or by saying that it contributes to the variety and perfection of the whole? The "solution" to this question can never lie in some theoretical answer that is forced to be dishonest and palliative from the outset. The solution can lie only in concrete human attitudes, in concrete human situations. The actual attitude bears witness to its own possibility and reality.

CHAPTER FIVE

Thoughts on a Nachlass *Fragment*

> Whoever gets the highest feeling from *striving*, let him strive; whoever gets the highest feeling from *peace*, let him rest; whoever gets the highest feeling from adaptation, *following*, obedience, let him obey. *Only let him become aware* of what gives him the highest feeling and not shun *any means! Eternity* is at stake![1]

This rather remarkable fragment from Nietzsche's *Nachlass* (1881) might strike one at first as a superficial, slightly desperate statement that has gotten lost in "limbo." At first reading, the gist of this fragment seems to be this: it does not matter what you do, whatever makes you feel good, go ahead and do it! If you want to strive, go ahead and strive. If you want peace, then rest. If you want to follow someone, then obey him. This interpretation, which is not only a possibility, but also the obvious one, seems to leave Nietzsche open to at least the following accusations:

1. Complete, subjective arbitrariness;
2. An anarchistic kind of "hedonism";
3. An extreme "psychologism" with no "ontological" foundation whatsoever, bordering on his own version of an "as-if" philosophy.

In this chapter, I should like first to take a look at the larger context in which this fragment appears, then consider the three points themselves and the dangers inherent in them, and finally to throw out the categories that Nietzsche and we ourselves with him inevitably set up in thinking his thought and attempt to see what is at the bottom of this fairly isolated, undeveloped fragment. For, surely, a thinker of Nietzsche's caliber must mean something more than "go ahead and do what you want to do," a "philosophy" that even the "man in the street" would regard as slightly less than profound or, in Nietzsche's own words, as being "not even superficial."

I

The larger context of our fragment reads:

> The political madness, about which I smile just as my contemporaries smiled at the religious madness of earlier times, is above all *secularization*, faith in the *world* and a putting the "beyond" and the "back world" out of one's mind. The goal of this political madness is the well-being of the fleeting individual. Thus, socialism in its fruit, i.e. those *fleeting individuals* want to win their happiness. Through socialization they have no reason to wait as the men with eternal souls and eternal becoming and future improvement do. My doctrine says: live in such a way that you must wish to live again, that is the task. You will anyway![2]

This larger "context" is what immediately precedes the fragment we quoted at the beginning of this chapter, and gives it its setting. Here, Nietzsche is struggling with the dichotomy of world and backworld, faith in the secular and faith in the religious. Whereas the general position of his thinking is to reject the "religious madness" (belief in the realm of Platonic Ideas and in the God of Christianity, among others) and attempt to affirm the "world," *this* world as the only reality accessible to us, he is here radically questioning whatever we usually understand by *this world*. Secularization, belief in the world, putting the "beyond" and the "back world" out of our minds is a *political* madness attempting to replace the religious one. In this political madness it does not matter whether one is talking about the fleeting individual or about the collective dimension of those fleeting individuals, their socialization and belief in a common goal attainable without the long waiting period for future improvement (belief in progress). The crux of this political madness, whether it emphasizes the individual or the collective dimension of those individuals, seems to be that it is a belief in a *false* "here and now."

What other kind of "here and now" is there? What is Nietzsche getting at? After rejecting "political madness" he advocates: live in such a way that you would have to wish to live again, you will anyway. This sounds as if he is directing our attention away from the present moment to the anticipation of repeating our lives (eternal recurrence), and then slamming down the lid of determinism on that attitude of anticipation with the words *you will anyway*. Here, Nietzsche is moving within the framework of a philosophical problem growing out of Spinoza, developing in Kant, and culminating in German Idealism, especially in Schelling for whom it was the prime question—freedom versus nature-determinism-necessity. And for Nietzsche, as for his predecessors, freedom means, of course, *human* freedom.

This is not the place to get into the intricacies, abysses and virtually insoluble problems posed by Nietzsche's absolutely central doctrine of eternal recurrence. Anyone who has tried long enough to grope his way around that philosophical terrain often returns from it as something far worse than the proverbial "burnt child" (certainly not the playing child of the three metamorphoses in *Thus Spoke Zarathustra*) and begins to fear that the element of recurrence is taking place precisely in his own desperate attempts to make sense of that doctrine. This leaves us with our question: What other kind of "here and now" is there, if we are not talking about the present, attainable happiness of individuals or of a collection of individuals? With this question we reach the second part of our enquiry.

II

Whoever gets the highest feeling from *striving*, let him strive; whoever gets the highest feeling from *peace*, let him rest; whoever gets the highest feeling from adaptation, *following*, obedience, let him obey. *Only let him become aware* of what gives him the highest feeling and not shun *any means! Eternity* is at stake!

If our treatment of the first part of the fragment was a bit sketchy, it was because we assumed that the dichotomy world–backworld (world of becoming, world of changeless being) is familiar to anyone who has spent much time with Nietzsche. But the options with which

Nietzsche presents us in the second part, if *really thought out*, are not really familiar to anybody. A bold statement. I believe that Nietzsche is getting at something that a later thinker, Martin Heidegger, developed in a more central and a more exhaustive way—the insight that *we do not know what man is*. Thus when we say of a philosophy, a doctrine, an attitude that it is *merely* subjective, *merely* psychological, what on earth do these words mean when we do not know what the "subject," the "psyche" really is? Therefore the emphasis in our present fragment does not lie in the words *striving, peace, following*, does not lie in a certain kind of "behavior" that "makes us feel good." The emphasis lies in the words *"only let him become aware," eternity is at stake*, and *rightly understood* (and this is difficult) in the words—and not shun *any means*.

We return to the three "accusations" mentioned before:

1. Complete, subjective arbitrariness;
2. An anarchistic kind of "hedonism";
3. An extreme "psychologism" with no "ontological" foundation whatsoever, bordering on his own version of an "as-if" philosophy.

1. Complete, Subjective Arbitrariness

The line between this accusation and the third is thin. One could say that the emphasis here is on an extreme individualism or even nonepistemological "solipsism," whereas the emphasis in 3 is on an extreme psychologism, the absolute lack of anything transcending man. In other words, here it seems to make no difference who is striving for what, who is following whom, what is meant by *peace.* All are "means" quite separable from the concrete goal desired (the only goal is "the highest feeling") and also totally isolated from any *Mitmenschen* (fellow companions). Everyone for himself, just get that highest feeling. That Nietzsche cannot mean only this becomes clear when we consider the doctrine of the soothsayer in *Thus Spoke Zarathustra* when he says: "All is empty, all is the same, all has been." Later, Zarathustra reformulates this doctrine as "all is the same, nothing is worthwhile, knowledge strangles." Nietzsche presents these "doctrines" as extreme dangers, dangers to be faced and overcome. Thus he is definitely not embracing the point of view that all is the same, that it does not make any difference what one does. He is not saying strive, *as if* striving were the key to the highest feeling and the right activity for everyone. He is not even being primarily pragmatic as if to say: if it works, it is *true* (the right way).

2.   *An Anarchistic Kind of "Hedonism"*

Admittedly we have so far said almost nothing about what Nietzsche means or might have meant, only what we believe he did not mean. Whatever "positive" suggestions we have will be attempted after a discussion of our three points of accusation.

"The highest feeling" as a goal suggests at first some kind of hedonism. The highest feeling must mean some kind of pleasurable feeling. It seems strange that the man who wrote so much on the metamorphic level of the lion (second stage of the spirit in *Thus Spoke Zarathustra*) who slays dragons with his courage, learns to live with

abysses, to destroy the old values that are at best superfluous if not life denying should write in this fragment
about a *feeling*. What kind of feeling can he be talking
about?

Joy. In "The Drunken Song" at the end of *Thus Spoke
Zarathustra*, Nietzsche tells us that "joy is deeper than
the pain of the heart, that all joy wants eternity—wants
deep, wants deep eternity." The German word for joy
here is *Lust*, obviously akin to our word *lust*, but by no
means identical with it in meaning. *Lust* usually means
some kind of pleasure or inclination, but these meanings
are far too feeble for the context and the tone of "The
Drunken Song." Nietzsche really means joy, and joy,
rightly understood, has nothing to do with hedonism.

The philosophers and poets have not had too much to
say about joy. The philosophers were, as a rule, more
interested in reason; and the poets, at least the romantic
ones, more concerned with sorrow or the transiency of
things. We might cite one philosopher and one poet as
exceptions to this generalization, Spinoza and Blake.

Joy is man's passage from a lesser to a greater perfection.[3]

Man was made for Joy and Woe
And when this we rightly know
Thro the World we safely go
Joy and Woe are woven fine
A Clothing for the Soul divine.[4]

What is perhaps most interesting about both of these
passages is the fact that they make joy so central to the
human being. Spinoza speaks of joy as the *passage*
toward greater perfection, thus emphasizing movement,

transition, and activity in a way not often found in his rather "Parmenidean" philosophy. And Blake makes joy—along with its counterpart, woe—finely woven clothing for the soul. Traditionally, nearly all of the emotions have been discussed in terms of opposites[5] because by definition an emotion *moves* us, takes us somewhere between the possible poles of "depression and elation."

3.   An Extreme "Psychologism"

To distance what Nietzsche means by the highest feeling from what is commonly understood as hedonism, we move on to the third point of accusation, that of extreme "psychologism." By this term, we mean the view that man is a purely "psychological" being with absolutely nothing transcending him: neither a god nor a higher possibility of his being. The contrast between this kind of psychologism and a possibility of transcendence is very clearly expressed in Heidegger's *Letter on Humanism*, where he compares his own view of human existence with that of Sartre. "Sartre: 'Précisement nous sommes sur un plan où il y a seulement des hommes' (Precisely, we are in a situation where there are only human beings). Heidegger: 'Précisement nous sommes sur un plan où il y a principalement l'être' (Precisely, we are in a situation where there is principally Being)."

Sartre's complete rejection of any kind of transcendence places man in a situation where he is "the sum of his actions," where emotions are human emotions and nothing else. Heidegger's central preoccupation with "transcendence," albeit not of the traditional kind, places man in a situation where he is principally defined as that unique being with access to Being, where his "emotions" *tell him* something about the nature of existence which reason alone could never do. In this context, Heidegger mentions joy, but he never gave it the kind of analysis that he gave to dread, which seems to have better lent itself to his philosophical intention.

The problem of transcendence in Nietzsche's thought is far too vast to be discussed here. But whatever Nietzsche meant by the *overman* and to an extent even by the *higher man* certainly points to a dimension of man that goes beyond the traditional concept. Given the wealth of statements about the overman—a wealth that sometimes borders on confusion—it is, of course, a gross misrepresentation to pick out a fragment or fragments that emphasize one aspect at the expense of others. But for our limited purposes, this could prove fruitful. "Goal: to *attain* the overman for one moment. For *this* purpose I suffer everything!"[6]

This fragment clearly indicates a *moment* of "transcendence," the overman conceived as a dimension of man that goes beyond man as we have previously known him. It is an intensified expression of Nietzsche's oft-repeated imperative: Man is something that has to be surpassed.

How is this to be attained? Whatever approaches an "answer" is to be found in the latter part of our initial, key fragment: "*Only let him become aware* of what gives him the highest feeling and not shun *any means! Eternity* is at stake!" Nietzsche speaks here of becoming aware, of becoming aware not just with one's rational intellect, but with one's whole being. Aware of what? Aware of something far more important than striving, peace or obedience, which are *means* and not even particularly central means, as the tone of irony (let him go ahead if that is all he can muster) in this fragment insinuates. In other words, let him become aware of just *"what"* gives him the highest feeling.

But, to formulate the question in a somewhat barbaric fashion: Just what is this "what?" I believe there is no explicit answer to this question in Nietzsche's writings, published or posthumous. But that does not mean that the question is invalid or even contrived. Every serious interpreter and student of Nietzsche knows that in dealing with this highly complex and enigmatic thinker one is eventually forced to make certain choices among conflicting aspects of his thought and ultimately to "go beyond" what Nietzsche himself said. This is nothing illegitimate, it is simply necessary in the case of any thinker, and especially in the case of Nietzsche. Otherwise, one is simply regurgitating ideas without enquiring into their implications and possible meanings. Who can state precisely and with absolute, exclusive authority, for instance, what Plato meant by the immortality of the soul or what Leibniz meant by his monads that are "windowless." One *must* "interpret." One must always reckon with the real possibility of going astray, of missing the mark. At best, one might succeed in coming up with a creative conjecture.

It is our contention that this "what" that gives the highest feeling points to the element of transcendence in Nietzsche. It distances him from all mere psychologism. The question of transcendence is highly problematic in Nietzsche, and yet it is unquestionably there. Any student of Nietzsche knows his rejectional attitude toward

Christianity, as well as any kind of otherworldliness most neatly exemplified in Plato.

HOW THE "TRUE WORLD" FINALLY BECAME A FABLE: THE HISTORY OF AN ERROR

1. The true world—attainable for the sage, the pious, the virtuous man; he lives in it, *he is it*. (The oldest form of the idea, relatively sensible, simple, and persuasive. A circumlocution of the sentence, "I, Plato, *am* the truth.")

2. The true world—unattainable for now, but promised for the sage, the pious, the virtuous man ("for the sinner who repents"). (Progress of the idea: it becomes more subtle, insidious, incomprehensible—*it becomes female*, it becomes Christian.)

3. The true world—unattainable, undemonstrable, un-promisable; but the very thought of it—a consolation, an obligation, an imperative. (At bottom, the old sun, but seen through mist and skepticism. The idea has become elusive, pale, Nordic, Königsbergian.)

4. The true world—unattainable? At any rate, unattained. And being unattained, also *unknown*. Consequently, not consoling, redeeming, or obligating: how can something unknown obligate us? (Gray morning. The first yawn of reason. The cockcrow of positivism.)

5. The "true" world—an idea which is no longer good for anything, not even obligating—an idea which has become useless and superfluous—*consequently*—a refuted idea: let us abolish it! (Bright day; breakfast; return of *bon sens* and cheerfulness; Plato's embarrassed blush; pandemonium of all free spirits.)

6. The true world—we have abolished. What world has remained? The apparent one perhaps? But no! *With the true world we have also abolished the apparent one.*

(Noon; moment of the shortest shadow; end of the
longest error; high point of humanity; INCIPIT
ZARATHUSTRA.)[7]

This rather marvelous, telescopic indictment of the
history of Western philosophy concludes with the statement that the high point of humanity begins after the
end of the longest error. We are now faced with the
problem of thinking this high point as something transcending man, which is yet not the Platonic Idea nor the
Christian God. Here it can be helpful to take a look at a
few of Nietzsche's relatively rare statements about
"god" that are *not* polemical, that attempt to speak about
god or transcendence in an utterly non-Platonic, non-
Christian way. *Transcendence* is by far a better word
here than *god*, because what it designates is quite neutral,
not limited to a personal god, a highest being, or a *causa
sui*. It could very well mean an act or a state of being.
Finally, we should be cautious about jumping to the easy
conclusion that, if Nietzsche rejects the traditional concept of god or transcendence, the only alternative is to
say that whatever he meant by *god* was a mere projection, a wish fantasy of man, exemplified in Feuerbach:
God did not create man, man created God. This would
be a cheap, misguided charge in view of the fact that
Nietzsche himself is keenly aware of this phenomenon
and already unmasked it with his central analysis of
"wishful thinking" (*Wünschbarkeit*).

Apart from Nietzsche's playful remarks about only
believing in a god who could dance and laugh, here are
some of his more serious, highly enigmatic statements
about god.

Latter-day man has employed his power of idealisation in regard to a *god* chiefly to make the god more and more moral. What does that signify?—nothing good, a diminution of the strength of man. For in itself the opposite would be possible: and there are indications of this. God conceived as an emancipation from morality, taking into himself the whole fullness of life's antitheses and, in a divine torment, *redeeming* and *justifying* them: God as the beyond and above of the wretched loafers' morality of "good and evil."[8]

God as the moment of culmination: existence an eternal deifying and un-deifying. *But in that not a high point* of value, but a high point of power.[9]

Let us remove supreme goodness from the concept of God; it is unworthy of a god. Let us also remove supreme wisdom: it is the vanity of philosophers that is to be blamed for this mad notion of God as a monster of wisdom: he had to be as like them as possible. No! God *the supreme power*—that suffices! Everything follows from it, "the world" follows from it![10]

The sole way of maintaining a meaning with a concept "God" would be: God *not* as the driving force, but God as a *maximal* state, as an apex (*Epoche*).[11]

Around the hero everything becomes a tragedy; around a demi-god everything becomes a satyr play; and around God everything becomes—what? Perhaps a "world"?[12]

In these quotations, Nietzsche is distancing himself from any possible conception of "god" as a person. That conception is precisely what he consistently rejects throughout his writings as the god of morality, of goodness and wisdom, who constantly "watches" man and judges him (as the *Gesamt-Sensorium,* as the ontological "voyeur" par excellence). Thus, whatever Nietzsche is trying to get at with the term *god* turns out to be some kind of high point of humanity, a high point of *power,* a maximal state and moment of culmination. To put it in an oversimplified and crude way, if "god" is not to be conceived as a being or eternal substance, we must think him as some kind of "force" or power accessible to man, accessible not to his knowledge, but "accessible" in the radical sense that man has existential access to that power; i.e., he can *become* that power or at least participate in it. Having existential access to "power" is an idea quite familiar to Eastern thought, particularly to Buddhism. The person who awakens to his "Buddha-nature" experiences an immensely liberating power at once elevating him above and immersing him in the suffering of life. Apart from many differences from Buddhism and apart from Nietzsche's own misunderstanding of Buddhism as a "religion of exhaustion," he is here close to Buddhism, a religion that does not believe in a substantial soul nor in a god. Buddhism states that life is suffering and it posits the demand and the means to get out of suffering. Similarly, Nietzsche is heralding the slowly increasing realization that human existence, just as it is, in its givenness, is simply intolerable without some kind of transcendence. His insight is that if God is dead, what we are "left with" is *not* just the inevitable, unchangeable "givenness" of what we think of as daily living. In other words, the *real* is not the given. What is ultimately real, in the supremely human sense, is our activity of transcendence and transformation. For this reason, for Nietzsche it is the artist who most closely approaches the overman, for precisely he can never regard what is given as what is real. There is no longer much we can do to salvage a real meaning for the words *transcendence, transformation,* and *creativity* that have become worn out from overuse and look anemicly sentimental on paper. But we have no other words for this phenomenon.

Plato, Nietzsche's favorite adversary, stated in the *Phaedo* that we must not "suppose that whatever cuases the most violent emotion is the plainest and truest reality" (*Phaedo*, 83c). In other words, what is most intense is not what is most real. But Plato was speaking of pleasure and pain causing emotions that rivet the soul to the body. Nietzsche's "highest feeling" cannot be equated with the kind of pleasure or pain that Plato is talking about.

There really is not too much to be said about what Nietzsche meant by the highest feeling, apart from emphasizing the fact that it is not merely arbitrary and subjective because the necessary counterpart and correlative or subjectivity, a world of static given objects, is completely lacking in a world of *The Will to Power*. But we can return to the question raised before of what gives this highest feeling: breaking out of the extremely limited dimension of what we have become habituated to consider "reality." All of Nietzsche's archetypes of the higher man do precisely this—the ascetic, the saint, and the artist.

Given Nietzsche's emphasis on the will, it is virtually impossible for him to speak explicitly of this breaking out in terms of some outside power (god). But many of his writings curiously belie the position that everything is effected by man's will.[13] If we could get rid of some of our habitual ideas about self and other, we could perhaps gain some insight into the possibility that the limitations of the self are not as inexorable as they seem and that what is "other" to that self is alien to it only in its limited dimension. In other words, the traditional question of whether "I" bring about the highest feeling by my own will or whether it is "given" to me, for example, by an act of grace, would have to be reformulated.

In conclusion, or perhaps rather in inconclusion, let us consider briefly what Nietzsche meant by his final words in our fragment: "Eternity is at stake!" What does eternity being at stake have to do with the highest feeling? And how can eternity be at stake at all? The most obvious interpretation would be to answer that if I am going to repeat my life endlessly, that life should be as "pleasant" as possible, because I am stuck with it forever. But this would be the political madness of the happiness of the fleeting individual about which Nietzsche smiles.

In an attempt to go beyond Nietzsche's inordinate reticence in speaking about the highest feeling—and who is not reticent in these matters if one is genuine—we might say that this highest feeling or moment of culmination is precisely something that *cannot* be repeated because it can never be lost. It breaks out of the dimension of what can be repeated. Thus, the phrase *Eternity is at stake* does not mean that my life will be repeated endlessly; but, rather, that becoming aware of what gives the highest feeling vaults us, so to speak, straight out of the dimension of endless repetition into something truly transcending the limitations of repetitive or repeatable reality. This is not a matter of conceptualization, but of experience. Hence, the words that sound strange and even alienating at first: "and not shun any means!"

CHAPTER SIX

Amor dei *and* Amor fati: *Spinoza and Nietzsche*

The aim of this chapter is to try to make some sort of comparison between Spinoza's *amor dei*, love of God, and Nietzsche's *amor fati*, love of fate. I do not wish to deal primarily with what Nietzsche thought of Spinoza (although that would be a valid and interesting topic), but rather to throw some light on the extraordinary phenomenon that both thinkers, independent of each other, *experienced:* the love of God or fate. I shall begin by centering on two questions: (1) What is loved? (2) What kind of "love" is involved here? A discussion of (1) will point up some fundamental similarities, perhaps identities, between Spinoza and Nietzsche.

Spinoza's God and Nietzsche's fate have at least the following qualities in common: neither is a personal creator-God, neither has anything to do with teleological purposes (and thus the world utterly lacks these), and both are strictly necessary and could not be otherwise in any way. Both thinkers stress the "immanence" of God or fate, and both could be called *pantheistic* in a qualified sense.

Of course, Spinoza's concept of God is more developed than is Nietzsche's concept of fate because God is the very core and foundation of Spinoza's thought. Novalis had called him a "man drunk with God" (*"ein gottbetrunkener Mensch"*). In contrast, what Nietzsche means by *fate* is intertwined with his basic ideas and is scarcely coherent or meaningful without them. In other words, God is the all-encompassing reality for Spinoza, whereas what Nietzsche says about fate is by itself not sufficient to delineate the originality of what he had in mind.

1. What Is Loved?—Spinoza

Having briefly stated what the two thinkers have in common—which will be the substance of this chapter— let us examine some of the unique features of Spinoza's God. Spinoza begins his *Ethics* by defining *causa sui*, the cause of itself whose essence involves existence, God; but this does not tell us what is unique about Spinoza's conception because it is the traditional definition going back to medieval times, with its ultimate roots in Greece. How to think a cause of itself concretely is problematic anyhow. It seems to be primarily a way of asserting the absolute independence of God; no one else caused Him.

Negatively speaking, God is not a person, and He does not create the world. The world follows from God with an immediate necessity that Spinoza describes in geometrical terms. Because we are concerned with the *naturans* and not the *naturata* right now, with God and not with the world, we shall focus on what it means to say that God is not a person. For Spinoza, man is not created in the image of God, rather man in his ignorance tries to "create" God in the image of man. Intellect and will in God are entirely different from human intellect and will in both essence and existence, so much so that all they have in common is the mere name.[1] Most important, God's intellect is spontaneous, not receptive, to use Kantian terms. What He thinks, He thereby creates. In God, intellect, will, and power are one and the same thing, and God's very essence is power.[2] If we can conceive of God as power and spontaneous intellect together, we approach the nonanthropomorphic and non*anthropological* dimension of Spinoza's God. He is absolutely necessary and cannot possibly be other than He is. Necessity and freedom coincide; to be free is to be self-determined from the necessity of one's being. This is what is distinctive about Spinoza's conception. The rest of what he says coincides more or less with traditional ideas.

2. What Kind of Love?

What kind of relation does man bring to this God whose intellect and will are so different from his that they have nothing in common but the name? Spinoza defines *love* as joy accompanied by the idea of an external cause.[3] *Joy* he defines as a man's passage from a lesser to a greater perfection,[4] stressing that joy is not perfection itself because that would not involve emotion. Joy is, so to speak, on the way to perfection. Emotions always move in a certain direction; they take us somewhere.

But what does Spinoza mean by perfection? He states that the most common way of speaking about perfection and imperfection is analogous to the way men talk about good and evil. They have an ideal standard in mind, say of a house, and according to how something does or does not measure up to this standard it is judged perfect or imperfect, good or evil. These are merely human ways of thinking and feeling; essentially they say nothing about the actual nature of what is being judged. Furthermore, such judgments make sense for Spinoza only in relation to man-made objects, objects of *techne*; they are totally inapplicable and inappropriate to things of nature, which just are as they are and cannot be otherwise.

Spinoza's own use of the word *perfection* (*perficere*) is closer to the nonjudgmental quality of being accomplished, completed, in this sense perfected.[5] In keeping with his constant and vigorous rejection of final causes, Spinoza states that things are not put in the world by God to attain some end that they (and He) lack, but rather they endeavor to persist in and increase their being, coming as close to perfectedness as possible. But perfection and reality are the same thing.[6] Reality, however, is God or nature or substance. Thus, man's relation to God is that of love, of increasing his being and thus becoming like nature: more free, more independent, more powerful because the very essence of God is his power.[7]

This love is intellectual. What does Spinoza mean by this? What kind of love can man have for God, particularly for Spinoza's God? The common image of the love of the child for the father seems totally out of place here. The Greeks had three words for love: *eros*, the love of the lower for the higher, closest to "erotic" love; *philia*, the love between equals, closest to friendship; and *agape*, the love of the higher for the lower, closest to selfless love, or even compassion. None of these seems to help us understand what Spinoza is talking about.

Let us try to throw some light on what Spinoza meant by *intellectual* love. Intellectual love arises from the third and highest kind of knowledge, which is intuition or immediate insight: "From the third kind of knowledge necessarily springs the intellectual love of God. For from this kind of knowledge arises joy attended with the idea of God as its cause, that is to say, the love of God, not insofar as we imagine him as present,but insofar as we understand that he is eternal; and that is what I call the intellectual love of God."[8]

This love of God is identical with understanding his true nature; it does not represent him as some present thing, but understands him, has a direct insight into him, in his eternity that has nothing to do with duration, time, or space. Understanding God in his eternity becomes love for God when man grasps his identity with substance and realizes that he is one of its modes. "The intellectual love of the mind toward God is the very love with which he loves himself."[9]

Let this rather schematic presentation suffice for now, and let us turn to Nietzsche.

3. What Is Loved?—Nietzsche

Nietzsche repeatedly speaks of *amor fati* as his innermost nature.[10] To begin with, it might be helpful to look at his distinction between "Turkish" and "Russian" fatalism. We should note that he makes no consistent demarcation between the terms *fate* and *fatalism* (and, in one passage, even *determinism*); they are interchangeable in his usage.

Turkish fatalism. Turkish fatalism contains the fundamental error of placing man and fate opposite each other
like two separate things: Man, it says, can strive against
fate, can try to defeat it, but in the end it always remains
the winner, for which reason the smartest thing to do is to
give up or live just any way at all. The truth is that every
man himself is a piece of fate; when he thinks he is striving
against fate in the way described, fate is being realized
here, too; the stuggle is imaginary, but so is resignation to
fate; all these imaginary ideas are included in fate. The
fear that most people have of the doctrine of determinism
of the will is precisely the fear of this Turkish fatalism.
They think man will give up weakly and stand before the
future with folded hands because he cannot change anything about it; or else he will give free rein to his total
caprice because even this cannot make what is once determined still worse. The follies of man are just as much a
part of fate as his cleverness: this fear of the belief in fate is
also fate. You yourself, poor frightened man, are the
invincible Moira reigning far above the gods; for everything that comes, you are blessing or curse and in any case
the bonds in which the strongest man lies. In you the
whole future of the human world is predetermined; it will
not help you if you are terrified of yourself.[11]

That "Russian fatalism" of which I spoke manifested
itself to me in such a way that for years I clung tena-
ciously to almost unbearable conditions, places, habita-
tions, and companions, once chance had placed them in
my way—it was better than changing them, than *feeling*
that they could be changed, than revolting against
them. . . . He who disturbed this fatalism, who tried by
force to awaken me, seemed to me then a mortal enemy—
in fact, there was danger of death each time this was done.

To take one's self as a destiny, not to wish one's self "different"—this, in such circumstances, is the very highest wisdom.[12]

Turkish fatalism conceives of man and fate as separate. Fate is something to which man is subjugated and against which he is powerless. This form of fatalism Nietzsche connects with traditional religion, with the demand for obedience to a power external to oneself.

To consider: to what extent the fateful belief in divine providence—the most paralyzing belief for hand and reason there has ever been—still exists; to what extent Christian presuppositions and interpretations still live on under the formulas "nature," "progress," "perfectibility," "Darwinism." ... Even fatalism, the form philosophical sensibility assumes with us today, is a consequence of this long belief in divine dispensation, an unconscious consequence; as if what happens were no responsibility of ours.[13]

Thus, the brand of fatalism that Nietzsche calls *Turkish fatalism* is basically an instance of man robbed of his autonomy and his freedom by a religion imposing a moral order on him from without. Let us now make the linguistic distinction that Nietzsche did not make and call this Turkish fatalism *fatalism* as opposed to what he describes under the term *Russian fatalism*, which we shall henceforth call *fate*. Fate is his own positive concept; fatalism is his polemical target. He loved fate, not fatalism.

To sum up, by *fatalism* we understand the traditional popular view of determinism; that man is completely determined by outside forces or, more important for Nietzsche, by an outside Force, God, and His moral decrees of good and evil. In the face of this, man can do either of two things: He can give up and cease to will or do anything, or he can devote himself to total caprice and arbitrariness, just aimlessly doing anything at all for the sake of doing something. Both of these options are fundamentally nihilistic. In contrast to this, Nietzsche's own conception of fate, expressed as *Russian fatalism*, lies in understanding oneself as fate.

What does it mean to understand oneself as fate? Apart from some abstract consideration of fate as a decree of God, as some sort of predestination, or as a kind of world order (*moira*), what Nietzsche really emphasizes most about fate is that things cannot be in any other way than they are. In this he and Spinoza are in complete and astonishing agreement. But in keeping with his more personal and poetic style, Nietzsche stresses the relation of the individual to fate. Because fate is not bound up with the Judeo-Christian idea of God, the question arises as to the "source" of fate, of who or what planned it—if indeed that is the case—and whether the individual is then free or determined. This latter question had become absolutely central in the nineteenth century, especially with Schelling. If you understand human freedom and its role in the scheme of things, you also understand the Absolute, nature, and essentially everything else. The question of freedom or determinism of the individual brings us to the second aspect of our inquiry, to the question of what kind of love is at stake here. But first we need to say something more about the source of fate and about what exactly fate is. The two questions actually blend into each other in Nietzsche's case: our two initial aspects, what is loved and what kind of love, collapse into one.

As we have said, one of the main traditional sources of fate would be a decree of God. This is obviously ruled out for Nietzsche. The alternatives would seem to be some theory of heredity or environment or, most likely, some inscrutable combination of both; or else some dimension of the individual that escapes sociopsychological analysis. The trouble with sociopsychological analyses is that they inevitably lack precision and reliability; there are too many "exceptions." For example, identical twins can grow up in the same environment and turn out to be quite different from each other. Heredity and environment are indisputably influences on everyone, but "influence" is too vague and inconclusive to deserve the name of fate.

So we are left with the question of a nonsociopsychological dimension of the individual. If fate is not to be understood as an external decree or power, then it must be grasped philosophically, not just genetically or environmentally, as something within individuals that molds them. "The highest state a philosopher can attain: to stand in a Dionysian relationship to existence—my formula for this is *amor fati*."[14]

The philosopher strives for a Dionysian relation to existence as his highest state. What is a Dionysian relation? It is a way of being or living, perhaps best to be conceived in the Kierkegaardian fashion where what matters is not the "what" but the "how." Kierkegaard says something to the effect that it is better to be an authentic pagan than an inauthentic Christian. Dionysus, the wine god, the god of intoxication, is the god of destruction and creation, of death and birth, of rebirth. To live in a Dionysian relation to existence means to live the creation and destruction that lie at the very heart and core of existence. The opposite of the Dionysian relation would be the Platonic quest for unchanging being that Nietzsche so vehemently rejects. Plato sought the eternal *eidos* or Form that has nothing to do with change and is inaccessible to the senses; Nietzsche absolutely denies the possibility of any static persistence and seeks "eternity" in becoming itself, in change, in creation and destruction, in eternal recurrence.

To live in a Dionysian relation to existence means to affirm the elements of creation and destruction as inherent in eternal recurrence. Nietzsche, as perhaps no one before him, discovered and expressed the paradox that one can create nothing new unless one affirms what is already there. And this "already-there-ness," this givenness, is what he means by fate.

The passage in *Thus Spoke Zarathustra* entitled "On Redemption" contains the pithiest presentation of Nietzsche's thoughts on the will's attitude of revenge. We do not want to go too deeply into that here, but only to state that revenge is one of several of man's extremely negative and crippling attitudes or feelings. Pity, envy, *ressentiment*, and hate would be other examples. Revenge is the will's antiwill against time and the "it was" or the past. Time is irreversible. What once happened I cannot undo or change; what once was, I cannot get back or regain. The past slips away from me off into some inaccessible "region" where I can neither get at it to change it nor possess it again. And from this "region" it intractably exerts its influence on my present situation; it affects me, but I am powerless to affect or change or regain it. It is out of my reach, forever; and yet it affects me.

Zarathustra states that the will must learn reconciliation with time, and something higher than reconciliation. The "it was" is a fragment, an enigma, and dreadful chance until the creative will says to it: "I willed it thus!" Having said that, the will can then say: "I will it thus! I shall will it thus!" Only when the will can affirm the past *as it is* is the will capable of willing creatively, not reactively, in the present moment and capable of freely willing the future:

> Has the will yet become his own redeemer and joy-bringer? Has he unlearned the spirit of revenge and all gnashing of teeth? And who taught him reconcilation with time and something higher than any reconciliation? For that will which is the will to power must will something higher than any reconciliation; but how shall this be brought about? Who could teach him also to will backwards?[15]

After these words Zarathustra falls fiercely silent, badly shaken. He is thinking thoughts that he apparently decides not to utter. Reconciliation with time occurs as willing back. This could mean either of two things: (1) to will backward in time, so to speak, turning time around, reversing it; or (2) to will things and events back, to will them to come again, to return. Both of these ideas are unusual, to say the least, and might strike us as impossible. No one that we know of has ever succeeded in reversing the direction of time in the sense of literally willing *backward*. This first alternative is so obscure that we are not even certain what it would *mean*, to will backward. But it is fairly certain that the general import is to change what has already occurred, to reverse time.

The second alternative at least makes more sense, even if it seems implausible. To will back things and events of my life means to will them *again*. This is Nietzsche's repeated question: Can I will that everything come again, can I will to live my life again and again exactly *as it is?* If I can say yes to this question, then I have a Dionysian relation to life. Strictly speaking, this does not reverse time, which continues to occur in a "forward" direction; however, nothing gets lost, it all comes back again. "My formula for greatness in man is *amor fati:* that one wants nothing different, neither forwards nor backwards nor for all eternity. Not just to bear what is necessary, still less conceal it—all idealism is falsehood in the face of necessity—but *love* it."[16]

4.   What Kind of Love?

The preceding passage may introduce the last section of our study, the question of what kind of love is at stake here. As we remarked earlier, the kind of love has really ceased to be a separate issue because the question of what is loved now completely defines the kind of love involved. One has a certain kind of love for a child, for a parent, for a man or woman, for an animal, for a piece of music, for a painting, for a landscape. They are all different feelings, which get lumped together under the well-worn blanket term *love*. But in each case the type of love is attuned to its "object," to what is loved. Thus, if the soul loves fate, the kind of love must be appropriate to fate, must be fate-ful—in other words, the soul itself becomes fate. This is a bold statement that we must consider very carefully. Let us look at a passage from *Thus Spoke Zarathustra,* entitled "On the Great Longing":

> O my soul, I taught you to persuade so well that you persuade the very ground—like the sun who persuades even the sea to his own height.

> O my soul, I took from you all obeying, kneebending, and "Lord"-saying; I myself gave you the name "cessation of need" and "destiny."

> O my soul, I gave you new names and colorful toys; I called you "destiny" and "circumference of circumferences" and "umbilical cord of time" and "azure bell."[17]

This passage dramatically expresses why we are no longer dealing with two separate questions: Fate is a name for the soul. The soul is placed in a cosmic dimension in that it is compared to the sun, just as Zarathustra often speaks with the sun and, like it, periodically goes under. This means that the soul is not to be understood in a personal or psychological way, but as part of the cosmos, indeed as a very important part. Playing on the word for necessity, *Not-wendigkeit,* Nietzsche gives it the very concrete meaning of "turning the need" and couples it with fate. The soul is fate and necessity, fate and turning the need. Of the other, more poetic, names for the soul, the phrase "azure bell" occurs earlier in the section "Before Sunrise," when Zarathustra speaks cosmically, this time with the heavens. He begins,

> Together we have learned everything; together we have learned to ascend over ourselves to ourselves and to smile cloudlessly—to smile down cloudlessly from bright eyes

and from a vast distance when constraint and contrivance and guilt steam beneath us like rain.

And when I wandered alone, for *whom* did my soul hunger at night, on false paths? And when I climbed mountains, *whom* did I always seek on the mountains, if not you? And all my wandering and mountain climbing were sheer necessity and a help in my helplessness; what I want with all my will is to *fly*, to fly up into you . . . [18]

and continues with the azure bell functioning almost as a leitmotif,

But I am one who can bless and say Yes, if only you are about me, pure and light, you abyss of light; then I carry the blessings of my Yes into all abysses. I have become one who blesses and says Yes; and I fought long for that and was a fighter that I might one day get my hands free to bless. But this is my blessing: to stand over every single thing as its own heaven, as its round roof, its azure bell, and eternal security; and blessed is he who blesses thus. For all things have been baptized in the well of eternity and are beyond good and evil. . . .

This freedom and heavenly cheer I have placed over all things like an azure bell when I taught that over them and through them no "eternal will" wills.[19]

Here, Zarathustra speaks of himself as of a heaven, a rounded, rooflike, azure bell that eternally protects and shelters everything in a joyful, eternal blessing. This poetic "imagery" for the soul is about as far removed from the Cartesian *res cogitans* as possible; the soul is not a separate substantial thinking thing, but rather a sheltering protection that grants eternal and blissful safety to all things. The sheltering heaven is not oppressive and opaque, but free and luminous, transparent light. The pure, deep heaven is an abyss of light. As so often in *Thus Spoke Zarathustra*, the imagery here is paradoxical. The heaven above is an abyss; to throw himself into its height is Zarathustra's depth; it speaks mutely to him. In another passage he says: Listen! for I want to hear you. The ordinary ways of thinking about things collapse here, and we are forced to experience them in a new way.

Finally, we need to look at the section in *Thus Spoke Zarathustra* entitled "At Noon," where Zarathustra falls into a unique kind of sleep while his soul remains awake. He speaks of and speaks to his strange, wonder-full soul, comparing it to a ship that has finally come into a still harbor. It is midday, and all is still; the world is perfect. Zarathustra muses about happiness, about how little is needed for happiness, and then corrects himself: more radically, precisely the very least makes up the best kind of happiness.

> Precisely the least, the softest, lightest, a lizard's rustling, a breath, a breeze, a moment's glance—it is little that makes the best happiness. Still!
>
> What happened to me? Listen! Did time perhaps fly away? Do I not fall? Did I not fall—listen!—into the well of eternity? What is happening to me? Still! I have been stung, alas—in the heart? In the heart! Oh break, break, heart after such happiness, after such a sting. How? Did not the world become perfect just now? Round and ripe? Oh, the golden round ring—where may it fly? Shall I run after it? Quick! Still![20]

The best happiness is experienced in a moment (*Augenblick*) that is so much the very least that it has nothing to do with time or duration at all. Zarathustra asks, What happened to me? What is happening to me? Am I not falling, did I not fall into the well of eternity? There is not distinction between past and present. This whole experience of noon is timeless, for when it was all over the sun stood in exactly the same place as when it started. It is clear that Zarathustra had some sort of experience of eternity. We cannot and need not go into the meaning of eternity here; what concerns us is the effect of that experience on his soul:

> "Who are you? O my soul?" (At this point he was startled, for a sunbeam fell from the sky onto his face.) "O heaven over me!" he said, sighing, and sat up. "You are looking on? You are listening to my strange soul? When will you drink this drop of dew which has fallen upon all earthly things? When will you drink this strange soul? When, well of eternity? Cheerful, dreadful abyss of noon! When will you drink my soul back into yourself?"[21]

Suddenly, Zarathustra becomes aware that his soul is strange; what we all take for granted as being the most familiar thing in the world, our souls, our selves, suddenly becomes totally unfamiliar, unknown. Who are you? Zarathustra asks his soul, and then asks the heaven, the well of eternity, when it will drink his soul back into itself.

To sum up the question of what kind of love is involved here, strictly speaking, it is less a matter of love than of a kind of identity. The soul not only loves fate; the soul is fate. Here the *is* is used in a transitive sense to mean the soul is, exists fate in much the same way that

Sartre said, "I exist my body." Thus, to say the soul is fate is not tantamount to saying flatly soul equals fate, soul is the same thing as fate; but soul lives out fate, soul is the living occurrence of fate. This identity also characterized what Spinoza was talking about when he said that "The intellectual love of the mind toward God is the very love with which He loves Himself."[22]

By way of conclusion, we shall attempt once more to clarify what Nietzsche meant by fate. First of all, he did not mean what most people mean by that word: he did not mean some kind of predestination. In this sense he is closer to the Greek idea of fate (*moira*), to the Greeks for whom the gods themselves were subject to fate, rather than to the Judeo-Christian idea. We shall gain a last insight if we take a look at the world-view that both Nietzsche and Spinoza rejected, at teleology. God and fate are, so to speak, the opposite or the negation of teleology, to use the *via negativa*.

If I have a purpose or goal or *telos*, it is something that I lack now and must strive after. This was Spinoza's objection to the purposeful "will of God," that His goals should be lacking to Him. Rather, Spinoza says, everything is already there and cannot possibly be otherwise. It must be just as it is. Nietzsche reached this insight when he realized that not only can we affirm the world process if we remove the idea of purpose from it; removing the idea of purpose first enables us to affirm the world process *as it is*, not as it ought to be. To consider the world process as it ought to be lands us back in the realm of good and evil, of Platonic backworlds, a world behind this world, judging our world to be imperfect and without value. Nietzsche strives for the innocence of becoming, becoming affirmed as it is with no reference to anything outside it. The innocence of becoming names the "world" aspect of fate, just as the soul names the "self" aspect.

> Question: does morality make impossible this pantheistic affirmation of all things, too? At bottom, it is only the moral god that has been overcome. Does it make sense to conceive a god "beyond good and evil"? Would a pantheism in this sense be possible? Can we remove the idea of a goal from the process and then affirm the process in spite of this—This would be the case if something were attained at every moment within this process—and always the same. Spinoza reached such an affirmative position insofar as every moment has a logical necessity, and with his basic instinct, which was logical, he felt a sense of triumph that the world should be constituted that way.[23]

If something is attained in every moment of the world process, no moment ever exists for the sake of another; each moment has its own necessity. In conclusion, we can say that both Spinoza and Nietzsche experienced fate as inner necessity, not as predestination or some kind of compulsion from without. To find and follow your inner necessity is to find freedom. The freedom of a painter is to find the inner necessity of his or her painting, to get it just right, neither too much nor too little, to get it the way it has to be. One could say the same thing for many activities in the arts, in acting, in writing, even in sports. Spinoza defined that thing as free which exists from the necessity of its own nature alone. And Nietzsche echoed this thought when he wrote, "The unconditioned necessity of all occurrence has no compulsion about it; he stands high in knowledge who has thoroughly realized and felt this,"[24] and, "*Fatum* is an elevating thought for him who comprehends that he belongs to it."[25]

CHAPTER SEVEN

The Innocence of Becoming

Two of the most central ideas of Nietzsche's thought, the Will to Power and eternal recurrence, attempt to describe the world process, the occurrence of world, in a new way. Nietzsche interpreters and scholars have sought to reconcile or at least relate these two ideas to each other in a way that yields a coherent world-view. Thus, for example, Karl Löwith found eternal recurrence to be essentially of Greek origin whereas the Will to Power has its roots in Christianity. In attempting to syncretize a goal-oriented process with one that simply repeats itself, Nietzsche was trying to bring back the Greek idea of repeating cycles of nature based, however, on the Judeo-Christian foundation of an irreversible, one-time course of history, ultimately an impossible and self-contradictory enterprise. Martin Heidegger attempted to fit Nietzsche into the metaphysical tradition as its completion by seeing in the Will to Power the essence of things and in eternal recurrence the existence of things. Heidegger did not see a contradiction between the two ideas but regarded them, so to speak, as different aspects or dimensions of the world, something that Nietzsche did not do.

The Will to Power and eternal recurrence are not the subject of this chapter, but they do lead into our topic without having been explicitly related to it by Nietzsche himself. The innocence of becoming stands singularly *unrelated* to most of Nietzsche's other main ideas, and thus it cannot be seen as a contradiction to any of them; nor can it be neatly fitted into the metaphysical tradition, let alone be regarded as its completion.

I am not playing these three ideas, the Will to Power, eternal recurrence, and the innocence of becoming, against one another with the intent of ending up with the innocence of becoming as the winner of some kind of competition; nor am I dumping them in the same metaphysical pot (which would almost have to be a cauldron). The first procedure would be a bad kind of "difference"; the second a bad kind of "identity." (Not only infinity is bad.) What I want to do is to inquire into what Nietzsche was talking about when he characterized the Will to Power as a new interpretation of all occurrence.

"Under the not undangerous title, 'The Will to Power,' a new philosophy or, speaking more clearly, the attempt at a new interpretation of all occurrence should find expression."[1]

The innocence of becoming is another, less-developed dimension of that same attempt at a new interpretation of all occurrence. I shall try first to deal with becoming and what it is free from for Nietzsche, and then turn to the idea of innocence, which will then lead me to the ideas of the child and of play. If I can scratch the surface of all this, I shall be more than content.

Becoming

This is the more familiar aspect of Nietzsche's idea of the innocence of becoming because he wrote about becoming from the very beginning and never lost his preoccupation with it nor his desire to vindicate and justify it. Briefly stated, he wanted to think becoming free of at least two things: (1) free of the relation to an existent ground, any kind of "being," outside the process of becoming, whether this be the Platonic Form or the witnessing creator god, and (2) free of subordination to any final aim or goal, whether this be salvation or some kind of nirvana, free, in fact, of any goal anywhere at all. The "positive" side of these two things, in Nietzsche's own words, what becoming is not free *from*, but *for*, would be (1) there is *nothing* outside the whole, outside this world; this world itself, as it is, is "perfect" in a non-moral sense and has no further need of anything, and (2) Nothing exists primarily for the sake of anything else. In short, the world is neither imperfect nor subordinate. Let us briefly try to clarify these two points further.

It is generally well known that Nietzsche rejects anything beyond or outside of this world. I am not so much concerned here with the whole Judeo-Christian morality issue as with the character of the world process. I shall get to the "human," if not ethical, dimension of the innocence of becoming when I get to the question of innocence as such. I do not mean to posit some kind of Cartesian dualism here. For Nietzsche, *everything* is in a state, no, a process, of becoming. More precisely expressed, everything "is" becoming. What "is," becomes. Innocence, on the other hand, applies to conscious beings and to the human dimensionof the world. A tree is neither innocent nor guilty. Of course, Nietzsche also means by innocence that this world is all right as it is, that there is no Platonic or Judeo-Christian standard to judge and condemn it; but the *philosophical* dimension of this points, again, to a conscious being trying to evaluate the meaning of all this, to the human dimension. As we go further, we shall find that becoming and innocence get harder and harder to separate.

With the emphasis on becoming, the innocence of becoming means that there is no unchanging being beyond or outside the world of becoming; and thus becoming is "guilty" of, is *lacking,* nothing. This means that "reality" is not somewhere else, not in an eternal, unchanging Form such as Beauty or the Good, nor in an afterworld or a backworld. The existence of the Platonic Form had meant that man could never achieve perfection, it was simply unavailable to him. He could only strive after it, but never actually attain it. When we look at the historical transformation of Platonic being in Christianity, the situation gets more complicated and more ominous. What Nietzsche objected to about the Christian god becomes more concrete when we consider the two ways in which God died. We leave out the less serious statement that he laughed himself to death. After all, Zarathustra says that when gods die, they always die many kinds of death, an echo of Shakespeare's line about cowards. On the one hand, God died of his pity for man, and on the other hand, we killed God. In reality, these two statements are not as contradictory as it might seem at first glance, but inherently complementary and reciprocal. In the section of *Thus Spoke Zarathustra* entitled "Retired," Zarathustra explains to the old retired pope, who had been looking for the first person Zarathustra met when he came down from his mountain, the old saint, that God's love for man had become his hell and ultimately had led to his death when he saw that it was *man*, not Christ, who hung on the cross. At a later meeting, the old pope shows that by now he already knew this (at their earlier meeting he did not yet know it) by further explaining that God grew weary of the world and of willing and one day suffocated from his excessive pity. The fact that God grew weary of the world and willing indicates that Nietzsche not only has Christianity and the Christian God in mind here, but also and perhaps more important Schopenhauer and his interpretation of Buddhism. For, although pity or compassion is a Christian virtue, it is *the* Buddhist virtue without which even the greatest wisdom is utterly useless.

Zarathustra then goes on to explain that, before God died, he had taken revenge on his creatures. "Too much didn't turn out for him, this potter who didn't finish his apprenticeship! But that he took revenge on his pots and creatures because they turned out badly, that was a sin against *good* taste."[2]

We have three forms of "god" in this section. Nietzsche seems to be demoting the Christian God to a kind of Platonic demiurge by saying that he had not finished his apprenticeship. Then he is saying that the God of the Old Testament took revenge on his creatures because they disobeyed him. Zarathustra remarks: Why did he not speak more clearly or give us better ears? And finally, as the God of the Old Testament grew old and turned into the God of the New Testament, he despaired of his botched-up handiwork and suffocated from pity.

Before going on to how we killed God, a short remark about God's suffocation is appropriate. This should remind us of the shepherd, and later Zarathustra himself, into whose throat a snake had crawled. The shepherd was choking on this snake, on "all the heaviest and blackest things." Zarathustra tried to pull the snake out of his throat in vain. Then "it cried out of him," bite the head off! The shepherd did this and lept up transformed, "no longer man." The shepherd *choked* (*würgte*) on something foreign that entered into his very body. In contrast, God *suffocated* (*erstickte*) from lack of air. I am not sure exactly what this means; I only want to point it out.

I now turn to the question of God's being killed. Now the emphasis of the question shifts from that of God being unable to live to that of man being unable to endure that this kind of God should live. What about God was so unbearable to man? And to which man was this God so unbearable that he killed him?

The man who killed God was the ugliest man. The German word for ugly means literally, "hateable" (*hässlich*). Zarathustra finds him in a valley of the realm of death, a valley where snakes go to die. He feels that he has been there before, which gives the whole scene an uncanny cast. Something is sitting in his path, something barely human, something unspeakable. Zarathustra is overcome with shame and quickly averts his glance. Then there sprang up from the earth a gurgling and rattling like the sound of water gurgling and rattling through clogged-up water pipes at night. From this noise finally arose a human voice asking the question: What is revenge on the witness? Finally the voice asks: Who am I? Suddenly Zarathustra realizes who the man is; he is overcome with pity, falls down, but gets back on his feet and speaks to him. "'You are the murderer of God! You could not bear him who saw you—who saw you constantly through and through, you ugliest man! You took revenge on this witness!'" The ugliest man answers:

"But he—*had* to die: he saw with eyes that saw everything, he saw man's depths and grounds, all his concealed disgrace and ugliness.

His pity knew no shame: he crawled into my dirtiest corners. This most curious, over-intruding, over-pitying one had to die."[3]

But far from feeling any kind of triumph over his deed, the ugliest man can hardly bear what he has done. In this he is reminiscent of an earlier figure in *Thus Spoke Zarathustra*, the pale criminal who can scarcely live with the *idea* of what he has done.

Both of these accounts of the death of God show that his pity either killed him or moved someone else to kill him. He died. Now there is no longer an everpresent, existing ground outside the world watching it. There is nothing outside the world. And this gives back to the world its wholeness, its self-sufficiency, its "innocence." The world is not to be punished because it does not measure up to being. There is no being. The world is lacking nothing. "Reality" is not somewhere else, it is right here in this world.

We now turn to point two about becoming, that it is free of subordination to any final purpose or goal, to any goal at all. When we say that becoming, that the world process has no goal, is this not tantamount to nihilsim, to the "uncanny guest at the door?" Must we not then say with the soothsayer in *Thus Spoke Zarathustra* that "everything is empty, everything is the same, everything was"; or in another formulation, "everything is true, everything is permitted?"

Not at all. The seeming paradox is that the absence of goals is so far from being nihilism that the very opposite is the case. It is the imposition of goals on becoming from without that led to the imminence of nihilism. The arch target Nietzsche has in mind here is the Judeo-Christian (and Persian) conception of history as the struggle between good and evil with the resultant triumph of good over evil. Something is intended, aimed at with history, that is, the defeat of evil. Whereas in our first point an eternally existing ground provided the standard by which to judge, condemn as guilty, and ultimately to punish the realm of becoming, in this second point the realm of becoming is again degraded and devalued to a *means*. It loses its intrinsic value. Nihilism threatens us because becoming, which is all there is, has value only for the sake of something else, again, for some static goal that, for Nietzsche, does not exist. This somehow reminds us of a Kafka story (there is more than one version) of a man who is summoned to a door and told to wait to gain admittance. The door, which has a guard, is meant only for him. He does not know why he has been summoned or what he has done. He spends his whole life waiting there, is never admitted, and finally dies.

Having stated that the absence of goals is *not* what Nietzsche means by nihilism, which is an historical phenomenon that we cannot and need not go into here, let us try to see what is *positive* about this absence. What, for Nietzsche, is the opposite of being goal oriented and having a purpose? The obvious answer would seem to be aimlessness, but that would be nihilism. No, the opposite of goal orientation or, if you like, teleology in general, is *Necessity*. This might sound a bit strange at first until we get a closer look at what Nietzsche means.

The question now arises of what, if any, kind of structure becoming has for Nietzsche. If he rejects teleology, does this then land him in some kind of mechanistic determinism? Apart from some of his so-called proofs for eternal recurrence, which do approach a kind of mechanism and which are not representative of the highest philosophical level of his thought, Nietzsche also rejects mechanism, along with teleology. We have not gone into this rejection of determinism and efficient causality in general because it has less direct bearing upon the innocence of becoming than do the concepts of an eternally existent ground and of purpose and goal. The alternative structure of becoming or the world process that Nietzsche offers to teleology and mechanism is *play*. As with his precursor Heraclitus, there is an obvious link between play and the child or innocence. We shall come back to this question when we speak of innocence. We shall also have to deal with the question of the relation of play and necessity. On the surface, they do not seem to be compatible.

We stated that the opposite of goal orientation or teleology was necessity. Nietzsche's conception of necessity is not deterministic, but is rather closer to Spinoza for whom necessity and freedom were identical. Necessity is *inner* necessity as opposed to being compelled by some external force. Nietzsche's attempt to affirm eternal recurrence, to affirm *everything as it is*, by being willing to repeat it exactly as is, gives expression to this inner necessity.

Becoming, free of purposes and goals, is *pure*. In the section of *Thus Spoke Zarathustra* entitled "Before Sunrise," Zarathustra addresses the heaven as the pure one, the abyss of light: "'To throw myself into your height—that is *my* depth! To shelter myself in your purity—that is *my* innocence!'"[4]

In contrast to the section "On Immaculate Perception," which, in addition to being an obvious parody of the Bible, is chiefly a rather devastating cirticism of Schopenhauer's will-less contemplation, Nietzsche is speaking with intense seriousness about what stains the purity of heaven. "'Together we learned everything; together we learned to climb up over ourselves to ourselves and to smile cloudlessly:—cloudlessly to smile down out of light eyes and miles of distance when constraint and purpose and guilt steam beneath us like rain.'"[5]

What can stain the pure heaven are passing clouds, the clouds of good and evil and of these half-and-halfs who can neither bless nor curse. Zarathustra states that he would rather sit in a barrel under closed heavens, rather sit in the abyss without a heaven, than see the light-heaven stained by passing clouds. He concludes,

> It is truly a blessing and not a blasphemy when I teach: "Above all things stands the heaven accident, the heaven innocence, the heaven chance, the heaven high spirits."
>
> "By chance—that is the oldest nobility of the world, I gave it back to all things, I release them from their bondage under purpose."[6]

We shall have to attempt to think necessity, play, and chance together in our second section. To conclude this section, we must briefly comment on what Nietzsche objected to about purpose and goal on a more individual level. He is, of course, not denying the general purposiveness of much human activity, but rather polemicizing against living one's life for the sake of some future goal. If I live my life for the sake of some future goal, whether it be some kind of worldly success or reward in heaven, I simply lose my present reality. I am not where I am. Not only that, I am then living a relation to an abstraction, to an idea, if not an image, and cut myself off from what is right in front of me. If I do this, there is absolutely no path leading to a direct affirmation of what is, which is Nietzsche's primary concern as opposed to the spirit of revenge or wishful thinking (*Wünschbarkeit, das Möchten*). "The meaning of becoming must be fulfilled, attained, completed in every moment."[7]

Innocence

Innocence is an important idea in poetry, literature, theology, and in a few philosophers, such as, for example, Kierkegaard, who gives a very subtle and masterful analysis in *The Concept of Angst*. The way most people use the term *innocence* is to designate a state of some kind of ignorance or lack of experience of something (an innocent girl, an innocent gambler). These two related meanings of innocence show innocence as a kind of basically untenable "not yet," a something that must be lost in the normal course of things. To *be* innocent would be to remain the same, if this is at all possible. Beyond these two meanings of innocence lies the more morally slanted one of not guilty. When we say that he was innocent of the crime, this does not mean that he did not know about the crime, but that he did not commit it. As the word formation shows, innocence seems to be primarily a privative concept: someone is lacking some kind of knowledge, experience or guilt.

Basically, Nietzsche starts out pretty much following this direction of thought. As we saw in the first section of this chapter, he wants to free becoming from the internal burden of goals and purposes. Gradually, the concept of innocence assumes a more important role in his thought, although this role is not made very explicit. The concept is always there, but it is never made central. Often it crops up as a phrase, as something he wants to "prove." It also occurs in a few places in his outlines for future "work" along with seemingly unconnected phrases, such as the will to suffering, chance, the creative, lightning.

Because we can safely assume that the *framework* for the question of innocence for Nietzsche is not theological, the question arises as to the context in which innocence makes its appearance. The remainder of this chapter will focus on the context and development of innocence, on the concept of the child and, finally, on play.

The initial context for the concept of innocence is an absolutely central one that runs throughout all of Nietzsche's writings: the relation between knowledge or consciousness and life. This context is very clearly articulated in an early work entitled "The Use and Disadvantage of History for Life," the second of the *Untimely Medita-*

tions. In this essay, Nietzsche is talking in the larger context of culture, but also in the narrower context of the individual. Thus, *history* has the dual meaning of a people's consciousness of its cultural roots and of an individual's consciousness of his own past, as the basis for possible action. In this essay, *history* basically means for Nietzsche "consciousness of the past." The question raised in the essay is, How does consciousness serve or hinder life? The main "value" here is life, not consciousness. This is quite consistent with Nietzsche's later views.

I quote the first section of the essay:

> Consider the herd grazing before you. These animals do not know what yesterday and today are but leap about, eat, rest, digest and leap again; and so from morning to night and from day to day, only briefly concerned with their pleasure and displeasure, enthralled by the moment and for that reason neither melancholy nor bored. It is hard for a man to see this, for he is proud of being human and not an animal and yet regards its happiness with envy because he wants nothing other than to live like the animal, neither bored nor in pain, yet wants it in vain because he does not want it like the animal. Man may well ask the animal: why do you not speak to me of your happiness but only look at me? The animal does want to answer and say: because I always immediately forget what I wanted to say—but then it already forgot this answer and remained silent; so that man could only wonder.[8]

The animal has no consciousness of the past or, for that matter, of the future either. It lives totally in the moment, in the present. Thus, it is neither bored or in pain (the two poles of Schopenhauer's life scale of feeling open to man); it is happy. Nietzsche goes on to say that the animal is unhistorical; it is every moment fully what it is. The same is true of the child "which as yet has nothing past to deny, playing between the fences of past and future in blissful blindness."[9] Man regards this happiness with envy "because he wants nothing other than to live like the animal . . . yet he wants it in vain because he does not want it like the animal."[10] One is tempted to say, "Aye, there's the rub." Man wants the happiness of the animal, but he wants it without the limitations of the animal. This factor of being "more" than the animal also applies to the child. The child's play "must be disturbed; only too soon will it be called out of its forgetfulness. Then it comes to understand the phrase 'it was,' that password with which struggle, suffering and boredom approach man to remind him what his existence basically is—a never to be completed imperfect tense."[11]

Briefly stated, Nietzsche discusses three kinds of life in this essay: the historical, the unhistorical, and the suprahistorical. The historical is subdivided into three kinds: the monumental (concerned with the future), the antiquarian (concerned with the past), and the critical (concerned with the present). The suprahistorical man does not see the meaning of life in the historical process, but for him "the world is complete and achieves its end at every single moment." This is Nietzsche's early vision of the overman. The suprahistorical man is above history; he lives in the present moment and is thus not conscious of self. This he shares in his own way with the animal and the child. The whole issue of innocence turns on what is meant by this phrase, *in his own way.* For obviously we cannot go back to being the animal, and we should not wish literally to remain children.

The possibly disruptive role of consciousness is a central theme in much of late nineteenth century literature. Whereas earlier writers had seen human consciousness as the very culmination of the whole of nature, some nineteenth century writers began to discover the crippling effect of a certain kind of self-consciousness. One of the most powerful examples of this can be found in a piece by Heinrich von Kleist, "The Marionette Theater." In a few pages Kleist portrays three episodes involving a marionette, a young man, and a bear, respectively. The first episode talks about the dance and shows how a jointed doll, with no consciousness, far surpasses in grace any human dancer who is more earthbound and cannot totally merge his consciousness with his body. Some of that consciousness remains, Kleist says, in his left elbow. The second episode describes a beautiful young man who happens, Narcissuslike, to see his own image reflected in water as he is standing in a certain way. The image reminds him of a well-known Greek statue, and he becomes enamored of that image of himself. He tries to repeat the stance but cannot. From that day on he loses all of his charm and grace. Once he became conscious of his grace, he lost it. The third and last episode describes a man fencing with a bear who is unbeatable. Not only does the bear parry every thrust, what is most remarkable, he never budges when the man feints or tries to trick him. Kleist concludes that no human opponent could have matched the bear in that. The best state in life is to have either no consciousness at all (the jointed doll) or at least no *self-consciousness* (the bear) or else the infinite consciousness of a god. We humans are, as Pascal already noted, in the middle.

If consciousness, particularly self-consciousness, is conceived as a potentially disruptive force, the question arises as to what kind of attitude or awareness is productive for life. We find the germ of an answer to this question in the third *Untimely Meditation.*

> Let us think. Where does the animal cease, where does man start? That man, the only one nature cares about! As long as someone desires life as he desires happiness he hasn't raised his glance beyond the horizon of the animal; he only wants with more consciousness what the animal seeks in blind impulse. But we all do this for the most part of our lives. Ordinarily we don't get beyond animality; we ourselves are the animals who seem to suffer meaninglessly.
>
> But there are moments *when we understand this.* The clouds scatter and we see how we, together with all of nature, press on toward man as toward something that stands high above us. Shuddering, we look in that sudden brightness, around us and backwards; the refined beasts of prey are running there and we with them. The monstrous restlessness of men on the great desert of the earth, their building of cities and states, their waging of wars, their restless collecting and dispersing, their running all over the place, learning from one another, their mutual trickery and stepping on one another, their screams of need, their howl of pleasure in victory—all of this is a continuation of animality; as if man should purposely be retarded and betrayed of his metaphysical propensity.[12]

All of man's activity has been a continuation of animality. But in the moments when we *understand* that we ourselves are the animals who seem to suffer meaninglessly, we see that everything, ourselves included, is striving for something more than this animality so broadly conceived. Notice that what Nietzsche is critical of about animality is not anything sensuous but frantic activity and competitive struggle, thus, a kind of human corruption of the animal.

This is, again, Nietzsche's early vision of a higher type of man. In the well-known three metamorphoses of the spirit in *Thus Spoke Zarathustra*, this higher type gets formulated as the outcome of a developmental process from the camel, the loadbearing spirit, to the lion, who in saying no to duty creates freedom, to the child. "The child is innocence and forgetting, a new beginning, a play, a self-propelled wheel, a first movement, a holy yes-saying."[13]

The child is innocence. This is an idea not unfamiliar to us. We find it in the poets, particularly Wordsworth and Blake. What can we say about the child that could further our understanding of innocence? In what does the innocence of the child consist?

It seems that there are two possible directions or poles to the child. We can say that, like the animal, the child is totally what it is. It is not divided, ambivalent, torn in different directions; it is wholly immersed in its being. But this total absorption can work two ways, depending on whether the child is opaque or transparent to its world, cut off from the world or open to it. There are children for whom the whole world is their ego; nothing else exists but their wants, demands, desires. This kind of child has not yet collided with the demands of the world or of anyone other than itself. It is simply opaque to what is outside of itself. After all, it is only a child, and for a time can get away with this attitude until it is forced to learn about something or someone outside of itself. Perhaps, or ideally, this kind of child is fairly rare. Then we have the child who is transparent to its world. This kind of child has not developed a sense of ego; it is blissfully lost in whatever it is doing, and there is nothing else in the world for it than just that. The child is a *totality*; it is not split, divided, or ambivalent; it cannot dissimulate or deceive. Whereas the motto for the camel was "thou shalt," and the motto for the lion was "I will," the motto for the child is "I am."

Nietzsche even uses the child to characterize God in a reference to Heraclitus' fragment about the world power being that of a child. "The phenomenon 'artist' is still the most transparent;—to see through it to the basic instincts of power, nature, etc.! Also those of religion and morality! 'Play,' the useless as the ideal of him who is overfull of strenth, as 'childlike.' The 'childlikeness' of God, *pais paizon*."[14]

The kind of childlikeness and innocence that we are talking about cannot be a pristine state; rather it must be something inevitably lost and then regained. As charming as children are, they do not represent an adult ideal exactly the way they are. No one can go through life without ever becoming aware of evil, deceit, and danger unless they are blind, deaf, and dumb in both senses of that word. As Kierkegaard pointed out in *The Concept of Angst*, initial innocence must be lost because otherwise one would forever be in danger of losing it. One would spend one's life on the brink of losing one's innocence. It is somewhat like catching the measles; once that is over with, one is immune and can forget about the whole thing. In his own version of a dialectic, Kierkegaard explains that we can speak of innocence only after it has been annulled (*aufgehoben*). Innocence comes into existence as that which was before it was annulled and now is annulled. In other words, it makes no sense to speak of a concept without reference to its opposite, to speak of an enduring innocence without reference to its potential loss. Similarly, a child is not aware of its innocence; if it is, it has already lost it.

Why is the child so important for Nietzsche? Why is it the highest of the three metamorphoses of the spirit? In contrast to the camel and the lion, who also have their function in the scheme of things, it is only the child who can create something new. Because the child is "innocence and forgetting, a new beginning, a play, a self-propelled wheel, a first movement, a holy yes-saying," it is unencumbered by the weight of the past. To be what we called *transparent to the world* means to be able to respond to what is there at the moment without thinking about self or what happened before. Preoccupation with causes and reasons why looks too much into the past; preoccupation with goals and purposes looks too much into the future; both modes of relating lose the present. It is the child who becomes or, rather, *is* what it is doing. Surely this is a mark of creativity, the focussed concentration on something to the exclusion of all distractions, to the exclusion of everything else. For the child, this is natural; for the artist, it is the result of discipline and practice.

The child is innocent in all three meanings of the word that we mentioned before. There is a great deal that it does not know, there are many things of which it has no experience, and it is guilty of nothing. To regain the quality of childlikeness—not childishness—means to know and to have experienced many things, but not to dwell on them, not to get stuck in them, become obsessed with them, or cling to them. What is fruitful about knowledge and experience, as Nietzsche points out in "The Use and Disadvantage of History for Life," is that they show us human possibilities. What was possible at one time, a Shakespeare or a Mozart, could be possible again in a new way. Thus, historical consciousness, knowledge, or experience do not have to have a paralyzing effect on us, although for Nietzsche they usually do, and the disadvantange worries him more than the use encourages him.

Real innocence is innocence regained. Nietzsche does not spell out for us in "The Three Metamorphoses" why the innocent child is the only one who is able to create. What is the connection between innocence and creativity? We know that as long and the will harbors the spirit of revenge in itself, as long as the will feels a counterwill against time and its "it was," it is powerless really to do anything, let alone create something new. Indeed Zarathustra says that man's best contemplation hitherto has been this spirit of revenge. Nietzsche shows us many "uncreative" figures in *Thus Spoke Zarathustra*, for example, the magician who can only act, but who is disillusioned with himself and must finally say "I am not great." I want only to mention one of the phenomena that stand in opposition to the creative child: the phenomenon discussed in the section of *Thus Spoke Zarathustra* entitled "Immaculate Perception." The target here is, again, Schopenhauer, who sees redemption and release from the hopelessly insatiable Will to Live in will-less contemplation of Platonic Ideas instantiated in art. We cannot get into the whole issue of Nietzsche's relation to Schopenhauer here, but we can highlight the question of creativity by referring to the imagery in this section of sun and moon. The pale moon is sterile, it even borrows its own light from elsewhere. It only lies there on the horizon, appearing to look without desire, doing nothing. Zarathustra speaks to the moon, chiding it for lacking "innocence in desire." The immaculate one, the pure knower, can never give birth even if it lies broad and pregnant on the horizon; it does not even nurture anything. In contrast, the sun loves the earth and the sea and approaches them with its glow. The love of the sun is innocence and the desire to create. Zarathustra asks, "where is innocence?" and answers, "where the will to create is. And whoever wants to create beyond himself has the purest will."[15] Thus, we see that innocence does not mean staying the same, remaining as you are, but precisely the opposite; innocence in desire lies in the will to transcendence, to create beyond oneself.

Staying the same, remaining as you are can never be an ideal of any sort for Nietzsche. What is so fruitful about staying exactly as you are? Obviously not very much. Thus, the stereotypical concept of innocence, that of remaining unknowing and inexperienced, is totally inapplicable here. If life is what must ever surpass itself, then man, as the form of that life most capable of transcendence, must surpass himself most of all. Nietzsche is speaking of the innocence of *becoming*, not of a *state*. Perhaps this is a dimension where his transvaluation succeeds. Perhaps he did not succeed metaphysically in subverting the Platonic framework of the realm of being and the realm of becoming. But—and this is more important if our prime concern is not metaphysics, reversing metaphysics, deconstructing metaphysics or whatever—he does go somewhere existentially by showing that innocence lies not in clinging to a precious, pristine state, but rather in change, transformation, even at times, loss, relinquishing something, destruction, going under.

In the intriguing, cryptic aphorism from *Beyond Good and Evil*, Nietzsche writes, "Around the hero everything becomes a tragedy, around the demigod everything becomes a satyr-play; and around God everything becomes—what? perhaps a 'world'?"[16] Whatever else this aphorism is suggesting, it is saying that from a certain kind of figure follows a certain kind of world. We might ask what kind of world follows from the child. This will bring us back to our initial question of the innocence of becoming as a new interpretation of all occurrence and thus to the conclusion of this chapter.

Simplifying Nietzsche—and this is in a sense doing an injustice to the richness and complexity of his thought, we could say that the Will to Power is basically a teleological interpretation of the occurrence of the world; the will is constantly striving to overcome new obstacles, to attain new goals. In some versions of eternal recurrence, particularly the attempts to "prove" it, eternal recurrence comes off a basically mechanistic. Finite force and infinite time are the constituents; the only role consciousness plays in this version of eternal recurrence is to pose the initial threat of being overwhelmed and crushed by the thought of repeating one's life down to the tiniest detail for all eternity. The innocence of becoming lends itself neither to a teleological nor to a mechanistic interpretation of the occurrence of the world, but points rather to play. What becomes around the child? The answer to this question has to be play. In contrast to mechanism, which, in addition to being deterministic, is basically for Nietzsche a product of the instinct of revenge,[17] and to teleology, which subjugates present reality to some distant, nonexistent goal, play is the highest instance of free activity. In *Ecce Homo*, Nietzsche writes: "I know of no other way to deal with great tasks than *play*; this is, as a sign of greatness, an essential presupposition."[18] And a note from the *Nachlass* reads, "new form of superiority: *play* with the holy."[19]

Play is diametrically opposed to the kind of playacting in which the actor indulges, a play that is totally geared to being observed and to show. But, above all, play is antithetical to the spirit of gravity who, among other things, would teach the child that self-love and self-affirmation are forbidden. In play, the child is free to create the new because it is unfettered by the past and not enthralled with the future. It plays in the magic of the present.

In conclusion, a word about the relation of play, necessity, and chance. These three are not as far away from each other as they might seem at first glance; in fact, they are very close. As for Spinoza, necessity for Nietzsche is *inner* necessity as opposed to being compelled from without and is therefore freedom in the true sense. Chance Nietzsche takes in the literal sense of what falls to one (in German, *Zufall*). "You speak falsely of events and accidents (chance). Nothing will ever happen to you but your own selves. And as for what you call 'chance,' you yourselves are what falls to you and falls upon you!"[20] To formulate it very succinctly, we could say that for Nietzsche necessity is the play of chance. This is expressed quite clearly in a *Nachlass* fragment: "Glorification *sub specie aeterni*—the highest fatalism, but identical with *chance* and the creative."[21] This was one of Nietzsche's visions of a new interpretation of all occurrence: the innocence of becoming.

CHAPTER EIGHT

Appearance: Nihilism or Affirmation

The concept of phenomenon in Nietzsche is filled with ambiguity and complexity. Some of this ambiguity and complexity stems from the fact that there is no counter-concept of noumenon or noumena. In *The Birth of Tragedy* Nietzsche still had a kind of metaphysical hangover from too much Schopenhauer and spoke of a thing-in-itself, the Primal Unity (*das Ur-Eine*). During this early period he also makes extensive use of the concept of appearance (*Erscheinung*), a term that pretty much disappears from his later writings. After *The Birth of Tragedy* Nietzsche polemicizes vigorously against anything smacking of a counterconcept to phenomenon, anything in itself. The often-cited passage from *Twilight of the Idols* entitled "How the 'True World' Finally Became a Fable" gives perhaps the most incisive formulation for the death of the form of thing in itself known as the *True World* or Platonism, a formulation not without humor.

HOW THE "TRUE WORLD" FINALLY BECAME A FABLE:
THE HISTORY OF AN ERROR

1. The true world—attainable for the sage, the pious, the virtuous man; he lives in it, *he is it*. (The oldest form of

the idea, relatively sensible, simple, and persuasive. A circumlocution for the sentence, "I, Plato, *am* the truth.")

2. The true world—unattainable for now, but promised for the sage, the pious, the virtuous man ("for the sinner who repents"). (Progress of the idea: it becomes more subtle, insidious, incomprehensible—it *becomes female*, it becomes Christian.)

3. The true world—unattainable, indemonstrable, unpromisable; but the very thought of it—a consolation, an obligation, an imperative. (At bottom, the old sun, but seen through mist and skepticism. The idea has become sublime, pale, Nordic, Königsbergian.)

4. The true world—unattainable? At any rate, unattained. And being unattained, also *unknown*. Consequently, not consoling, redeeming or obligating: how can something unknown obligate us? (Gray morning. The first yawn of reason. The cockcrow of positivism).

5. The 'true' world—an idea which is no longer good for anything, not even obligating—an idea which has become useless and superfluous—*consequently*, a refuted idea: let us abolish it! (Bright day; breakfast; return of *bon sens* and cheerfulness; Plato's embarassed blush; pandemonium of all free spirits.)

6. The true world—we have abolished. What world has remained? The apparent one perhaps? But no! *With the true world we have also abolished the apparent one.* (Noon; moment of the briefest shadow; end of the longest error; high point of humanity; INCIPIT ZARATHUSTRA.)[1]

For Nietzsche there is no such thing as being, the Platonic Form, or the god of traditional philosophy and theology. Becoming and appearance, the two concepts most traditionally opposed to being, are what make up this world, the only world that exists. The fact that there is no such thing as being, but only becoming, precisely elevates appearance to a stature of paramount importance.

Nietzsche seldom uses the term *Phänomene* (phenomena), a perfectly good German word in the current philosophical terminology of his time. Aside from passages speaking about the *Phänomenalismus* (phenomenalism) and *Phänomenalität* (phenomenality) of the inner world and an occasional statement about the world of phenomena and the reality of phenomena, the term occurs infrequently. Basically, then, we are dealing with two German terms: *Erscheinung*, which means appearance; and *Schein*, which means semblance. The whole problematic of the ambiguity of the term *appearance* is expressed in these two terms. An appearance can be something deceptive, masking the true state of affairs. For example, he appeared to be healthy, but in reality he was quite ill. Then again, appearance can indicate or can be something real, something that actually appeared and took place. For example, he appeared in the doorway.

Even though, or perhaps especially because, there is no noumenon or thing in itself for Nietzsche, the ambiguity inherent in the word *appearance* permeates all of his philosophy. Within the scope of this chapter, it is obviously not possible to treat this problem exhaustively; I shall confine myself to trying briefly to clarify what Nietzsche meant by *appearance* by simplifying the plethora of his remarks to two possible levels of meaning; levels, however, that are not completely separable. Linguistically, Nietzsche himself makes no clear-cut distinction between *Erscheinung* (appearance) and *Schein* (semblance); he uses them both predominantly in the sense of semblance or illusion, which, however, is all that exists. In the earlier writings *Erscheinung* predominates, because he still has the "thing in itself" (*Ding an sich*) in mind. Later on, the term *Schein* predominates almost exclusively.

Let us examine the first level of meaning: passages like the one cited where Nietzsche says that when the true world is untenable, the phrase *apparent world* loses its meaning. If there is no true world, there is no apparent world either; the distinction collapses. Many of these passages concentrate on unmasking the so-called inner world of consciousness as the most apparent or illusory of all; Nietzsche's critique of true and stable things in themselves by no means confines itself to the outer realm of empirical objects.

Let us now examine the second level of meaning: passages where art as semblance or illusion becomes the "true" reality. Sometimes art is conceived as overcoming an objective "truth" that is potentially nihilistic.

In *Thus Spoke Zarathustra* Nietzsche speaks of the three metamorphoses of the spirit. Taking these as our guide, we might say that Nietzsche left the camel, the stage of duty, behind very quickly. Therefore what we are dealing with in Nietzsche is the lion, the stage of destroying old values, and the child, the stage of creating something new. Keeping in mind our topic of phenomena, the question becomes to what extent Nietzsche remained a diagnostician of philosophy, religion, and culture, and to what extent he succeeded in offering a way out of the pessimism and nihilism that he diagnosed. The stage of the lion would correspond to Nietzsche's statements that there is no true world, no thing in itself. The stage of the child would correspond to the question of what is now to be done in this world unmasked and liberated from the false preconceptions we have insinuated into it.

Undoubtedly the preponderance of Nietzsche's genius lies in his unswerving, uncompromising diagnosis of Western philosophical, religious, and cultural values. In a rather global way this diagnosis extends to the Eastern religions of Hinduism and Buddhism as well.

Returning to "How the True World Finally Became a Fable," we can say that there is no permanent, ready-made reality behind or above the flux of appearances. There is no "reality" already "there" waiting for us.

This is what Nietzsche calls *nihilism*, the "uncanny guest at the door."

> What does nihilism mean? *That the highest values devaluate themselves.* The aim is lacking; "why?" finds no answer. *Radical nihilism* is the conviction of an absolute untenability of existence when it comes to the highest values one recognizes; plus the realization that we lack the least right to posit a beyond or even an in itself of things that might be "divine" or morality incarnate.[2]

Nietzsche traces the roots of nihilism back to the Christian-moral interpretation of the world. Christianity is "Platonism for the people." What is the significance of all this for the question of phenomena, of appearances? According to Nietzsche, the Platonistic-Christian view posited a transcendent "backworld" (*Hinterwelt*) that was eternal, perfect, and provided a standard by which to judge (or misjudge) "this" world. The transcendent backworld, the true world, which for Nietzsche never existed but was rather, the projection of dissatisfaction with this world of "wishful thinking" (*Wünschbarkeiten*), imposed all the "false" values upon this world, thus robbing this world of whatever value, autonomy, and power it originally possessed. Now Nietzsche proclaims that the true world no longer exists, that God has died. We are left with this world, devalued and stripped of all value and power. Thus Nietzsche wanted a transvaluation of all values (*Umwertung aller Werte*).

The world consists of nothing but appearances, but these appearances have been deprived of whatever value and creative power they might have once possessed. If the true world no longer exists, phenomena could regain new creative possibilities. But this cannot happen of itself. As things stand, all we have are devalued, impoverished, flattened-down phenomena. In short, we do not even have the phenomenal world as it "really" is, but rather a phenomenal world upon which we have imposed the devaluating judgments of Platonism-Christianity. Strictly speaking, there is for Nietzsche no such thing as the phenomenal world as it "really" is, because that would imply more stability and permanence in the world than there actually is. But the phenomenal world, as we now perceive it, is a falsified world. "What is 'appearance' (*Schein*) for me now? Certainly not the opposite of some essence: what could I say about any essence except to name the attributes of its appearance! ... Appearance is for me that which lives and is effective."[3]

Excursion

If we turn briefly to Nietzsche's own favorite of all his books, *Thus Spoke Zarathustra*, we might consider an intriguing facet to the problematic of phenomen*on*, not phenomen*a*. In the crucial section entitled "On Vision and Enigma," Zarathustra encounters a phenomenon, *ein Gesicht*, literally a face or countenance. This phenomena is not just a vision in the ordinary, weak sense of the word, but something actually seen, something countenanced. It shows itself in the most direct way possible in a momentous encounter. It is a kind of *singulare tantum*, totally unique.

What is this phenomenon? It is a "poetic" phenomenon, a "poetic" presentation of Nietzsche's thought of eternal recurrence that transcends ordinary, everyday conceptions of space and time. Breifly stated, past and future meet in the general gateway of the present moment; all time and space come to presence in the eternal present moment. This is an utterly unique kind of phenomenon, one whose meaning is not immediately apparent. It requires thoughtful interpretation and sensitive response. But this countenance, too, is a phenomenon in an important and significant sense and should not be entirely left out in a discussion of phenomena in Nietzsche.

To gain any kind of clarity on the subject of phenomenon, one simply has to cut through some of Nietzsche's inconsistencies in terminology, relying more on the context of what he is saying, rather than on whether he is using the term *semblance* (*Schein*) or *appearance* (*Erscheinung*). The basic question here does not lie in a distinction between semblance and appearance simply because Nietzsche makes no such consistent distinction, as well he might and perhaps should have. The basic question is, How do we experience these phenomena, what are we to do with them? Do we despair over the fact that there is nothing but appearance and becoming, succumb to nihilism and resign ourselves to a passive acceptance of our fate? Or do we experience the lack of "being," even the lack of stable *things*, let alone values, in the world as a dimension of freedom, as a challenge to our creativity? In the first case, we are nihilists; in the second case, artists. "'Reason' is the cause of our falsification of the evidence of the senses. Insofar as the senses show becoming, passing away, change, they do not lie. . . . But Heraclitus will always be right in this, that being is an empty fiction. The 'apparent' world is the only one: the 'real' world has only been lyingly added . . ."[4]

Nietzsche spent a great deal of time analyzing and diagnosing nihilism in its various forms, passive and active, European and Eastern. However, he gave us not only a diagnosis, but to some extent a prescription as well. That prescription is art, art so broadly conceived that it not only encompasses art works but, more important, the shaping of "reality" and phenomenon as well. Because with regard to truth Nietzsche oscillates between saying that there is no truth and saying that the truth is something terrible, truth simply ceases to be his major consistent concern. If there is to be such a thing as truth, we must form and shape reality and phenomena. In the terminology of Nietzsche's early work, *The Birth of Tragedy*, we must give Apollinian form to Dionysian chaos. Either way, what is crucial is art.

> We possess *art* lest we *perish of the truth*.[5]

> The belief that the world as it ought to be *is*, really exists, is a belief of the unproductive who do *not desire to create*

a world as it ought to be. They posit it as unavailable, they seek ways and means of reaching it.

"Will to truth"—*as the impotence of the will to create.*[6]

What happens to phenomena if they are not something that appears of themselves and are true? They become a kind of challenge and potentiality for creativity. They are not already there and accessible, but must first be shaped by us. For the person with the courage to accept this challenge who is not frightened by the fact that phenomena do not come "ready-made,"this offers the possibility of tremendous freedom.

> Why *not*? It is nothing more than a moral prejudice that truth is worth more than semblance (Schein); it is, in fact, the worst proved supposition in the world. *So* much must be conceded: there could have been no life at all except on the basis of perspective estimates and semblances (*Scheinbarkeiten*); and if, with the virtuous enthusiasm and stupidity of many philosophers, one wished to do away altogether with the "seeming world" (*die 'scheinbare Welt*)—well, granted that *you* could do that,—at least nothing of your "truth" would thereby remain![7]

The question of whether we are nihilists or artists becomes a question of power, this much misunderstood and rather dangerous concept so important to Nietzsche. After all, if, as Nietzsche asserts, life is the will to power and nothing else, then power becomes of extreme importance with regard to life and the affirmation of life. Power for Nietzsche has essentially nothing to do with political power or any sort of power over others.

In Nietzsche's radically dynamic view of the world, whatever does not increase in power automatically decreases. There is no possible *stasis*, no status quo. This is strangely reminiscent of, in many ways, a kindred spirit of Nietzsche's, a thinker whom he admired more than most: Spinoza. In a nonmoralistical way Spinoza calls *good* whatever increases our power of action. Nietzsche also relates power to the self, speaking not of power over something or someone external, but of power to do something, of being empowered. This highest power is power over oneself, or discipline. Surely discipline is essential to any kind of human enterprise, and absolutely so to the artist. "Overcoming of philosophers through the destruction of the world of being: intermediary period of nihilism: before there is yet present the strength to reverse values and to deify becoming and the apparent (*scheinbare*) world as the only world, and to call them good."[8]

According to Nietzsche, the philosophers looked at the world passively and objectively. They reified and substantialized the flux of becoming. In contrast, the artist is active; he does not contemplate objects, but creates new forms. In so doing, he transforms the world and himself.

> In this condition[9] one enriches everything out of one's own abundance: what one sees, what one desires, one sees swollen, pressing, strong, overladen with energy. The man in this condition transforms things until they mirror his power—until they are reflections of this perfection. This *compulsion* to transform into the perfect is—art. Even all that which he is not becomes for him nonetheless part of his joy in himself; in art man takes delight in himself as perfection.[10]

Among other things, this passage emphasizes the inseparability and wholeness of man and all things, of man and world. When he is in an "artistic" condition, a condition of intoxication, man experiences the oneness of himself and the world; not passively in some sort of mystic absorption, but actively in transforming everything into reflections of his power and perfection.

> What alone can *our* teaching be? That no one *gives* a human being his qualities: not God, not society, not his parents or ancestors, not *he himself.* . . . No one is accountable for existing at all, or for being constituted as he is, or for living in the circumstances and surroundings in which he lives. The fatality of his nature cannot be disentangled from the fatality of all that which has been and will be. . . . One is necessary, one is a piece of fate, one belongs to the whole—there is nothing which could judge, measure, compare, condemn the whole. . . . But nothing exists apart from the whole![11]

According to Nietzsche, we can place the responsibility or blame for ourselves neither on heredity, nor on environment, nor on ourselves as isolatable individuals. Each person is a necessary ingredient of the whole, which cannot be judged or even compared with anything because there is no vantage point outside the whole from which to do so.

Although Nietzsche participated to some extent in the nineteenth-century cult of the artist, and particularly the genius, his keen perception was nevertheless not blinded by mindless admiration. His later vehement rejection of Wagner is ample evidence of this. Fundamentally, Nietzsche's concern is not with art alone, although the artist is the type of higher man who comes closest to approximating the overman, the kind of human being Nietzsche hoped would be able to take the place of the old god. Nietzsche's crucial concern lies in the question of affirmation, of affirmation of life. His whole philosophical life was spent doing battle with his early mentor, Schopenhauer and, in a different way, Wagner. Nietzsche finally came up with a kind of "answer" to Schopenhauer's pessimism and doctrine of the denial of the will to live. What is ultimately at stake is our "attitude" toward life. Attitude is not intended here in a merely psychological sense, but more in the sense of a *stance* toward life, the posture with which we encounter it. Therefore the question here is neither merely psychological nor physical, but involves the whole *being* of the human being,

> *What is romanticism?*—In regard to all aesthetic values, I now employ this fundamental distinction: I ask in each individual case "has hunger or superabundance become creative here?" At first sight, another distinction might seem more plausible—it is far more obvious—namely the distinction whether the desire for rigidity, eternity, *"being"* has been the cause of creation, or rather the desire for destruction, for change, for *becoming*. But both kinds of desire prove, when examined more closely, to be ambiguous and interpretable according to the scheme mentioned above, which, I think, is to be preferred.
>
> The desire for destruction, change, becoming can be the expression of an overfull power pregnant with the future (my term for this, as is known, is the word "Dionysian"); but it can also be the hatred of the ill-constituted, disinherited, underprivileged, which destroys,

has to destroy, because what exists, indeed existence itself, all being itself enrages and provokes it.

"Eternalization," on the other hand, *can* proceed from gratitude and love—an art of this origin will always be an art of apotheosis, dithyrambic perhaps with Rubens, blissful with Hafiz, bright and gracious with Goethe, and shedding a Homeric aureole over all things—but it can also be that tyrannic will of a great sufferer who would like to forge what is most personal, individual, and narrow—most idiosyncratic—in his suffering, into a binding *law* and compulsion, taking revenge on all things, as it were, by impressing, forcing and branding into them his image, the image of his torture. The latter is romantic pessimism in its most expressive form, whether as Schopenhauerian philosophy of will or as Wagnerian music.[12]

The distinction hunger-superabundance undercuts even what has been taken as the most basic philosophical distinction: being-becoming. Nietzsche is not talking about the world apart from the human being nor, for that matter, about the human being apart from the world, but about the whole.

What matters is the *motive* in the root sense of what moves us. The desire for destruction and change can be Dionysian; destruction is essential to the creation of anything new. Dionysus must die in order to be reborn. Then again, the desire for destruction can stem from a smouldering rage and resentment against life itself. A man miserable and unhappy with *his* life would like to destroy *all* life. If he cannot be happy, then no one else should be able to be happy either. This is perilously close to Schopenhauer's much yearned-for denial of the will to live. Life is at bottom something despicable, full of suffering and frustration. The term *frustration* stems from the Latin *frustra,* which means "in vain." Phrases such as "all is in vain, nothing is worthwhile, all is the same" recur in slightly different formulations throughout Nietzsche's writings. They embody the threatening danger of nihilism that he was confronting. If this is the way things are, nothing we can possibly do has any meaning or makes any difference. Under these circumstances this would indeed be "the worst of all possible worlds."[13]

Similarly, the desire to eternalize, perpetuate, or preserve something can stem from the love of beauty, this term, once so absolutely central, that is fast disappearing from our meaningful vocabulary. In the *Phaedo* Plato stated that "through the Beautiful the beautiful is beautiful." Today's logicians might well dismiss this statement as an example of tautology. And Keats still was able to say, "beauty is truth, truth beauty,—that is all ye know on earth, and all ye need to know." But beauty has become increasingly difficult to find or to speak about. Certainly contemporary art seldom has anything to do with beauty. Guernica is not beautiful; Beckett's plays are not beautiful.

However, the desire to eternalize can also stem from an individual's profound suffering from himself, from the need to immortalize his very suffering by forcing the image of his torture on everything. As was the case in the negative instance of the desire for destruction, the motive here is again *revenge,* this most terrible of all emotions that Nietzsche uncovered and laid bare. Revenge does not simply entail one person attempting to get back at another; rather, the most profound dimension of revenge is that described in *Thus Spoke Zarathus-*

tra, the revenge against time and time's "it was," revenge against finitude itself.

In some sense, the whole distinction of passivity-activity needs to be rethought. Nietzsche utterly rejects passivity as a kind of nihilistic resignation and exhaustion of the will. The opposite of this is certainly some kind of "activity." There is a profound ambivalence in Nietzsche as to what kind of activity is at stake here. With his insistent emphasis on the will, a strong element of "voluntarism" in his thought is undeniable. And yet Nietzsche's emphasis on art and creativity offers another dimension to the question of activity. Artistic creativity does involve discipline, but it is by no means a matter of will alone. Rather it is a kind of activity that springs from a *response* to the real. Thus it transcends the passive-active dichotomy conceived as resignation-voluntarism and enters another dimension. A response is nothing passive or reactive; on the contrary, it is a spontaneous activity that we do not and absolutely *can*not force. *Sponte* means "of itself." Not artificially produced, willed or forced by us, something simply happens. If one were unable to respond to another person or to a piece of music or a poem or to a beautiful landscape, life would be impoverished indeed. Only from the dimension of spontaneous response is much of *Thus Spoke Zarathustra* accessible. It is not a matter of chance that Keiji Nishitani, undeniably one of Japan's greatest thinkers, considered it "scripture."

What is the significance of this for phenomena? What is the relation of affirmation or negation for phenomena? Ultimately, for Nietzsche phenomena are not what appears, but what is formed and created. *What* is formed and created depends upon our active or passive relation to the world. The quality of this relation is the crux of the whole question of the meaning or meaninglessness of life.

> Art and nothing but art! It is the great means of making life possible, the great seduction to life, the great stimulant of life. . . .
>
> One will see that in this book[14] pessimism, or to speak more clearly, nihilism, counts as "truth." But truth does not count as the supreme value, even less as the supreme power. The will to appearance (*Schein*), to illusion, to deception, to becoming, and change (to objectified deception) here counts as more profound, primeval, "metaphysical" than the will to truth, to reality, to mere appearance (*Schein*). . . . In this way, this book is even antipessimistic: that is, in the sense that it teaches something that is stronger than pessimism, "more divine" than truth: *art*.
>
> . . . Perhaps he has experience of nothing else!—that art is *worth more* than truth. . . .
>
> "Art as the real task of life, art as life's metaphysical activity—"[15]

CHAPTER NINE

The Other Nietzsche

Everyone seems to have his or her own Nietzsche. There are various versions of Nietzsche belonging to literary criticism and also to musicologists. There is the Nietzsche distortion perpetrated by the Nazis. There was a lot of pre-Kaufmann nonsense about the Nietzsche who was mad from the outset and produced nothing but the ravings of a madman. More recently and more philosophically, the two main continental interpretations have been expressed by the French, neo-Freudian, and Derridian line, and the German, Heideggerian line that sees in Nietzsche the completion of the history of metaphysics. These two interpretations are valid in varying degrees. What I should like to explore a bit in this chapter is a Nietzsche relatively untouched by all of these interpretations. It is not the whole of Nietzsche by any means; but it is there. I shall call the other Nietzsche: Nietzsche the poetic mystic.

A word about the terms *poetic* and *mystic* is appropriate here. Justifying the exclusion of poetry from a well-ordered state, Plato says that there was an ancient quarrel between poetry and philosophy. Poetry and the arts in general appealed to and strengthened the irrational side of man, nourishing the feelings and impairing the reason. Well, it seems that philosophy has pretty much won that quarrel. Few philosophers turn to poetry to find "truth." And yet Plato himself was a poet, as was Nietzsche. There have always been a few thinkers willing and able to listen to the inspiration of the poets. Surely there is a great deal of truth and insight into human nature in, for example, the works of Shakespeare. So much for the term *poetic.*

The word *mystic* has fared even worse. Not only are we dealing with a harmless bard enchanted with beauty as was the case with the poet; we are now faced with someone utterly devoid of reason *and* sense and who, to compound the chaos, is unable to state anything coherently about what he has supposedly experienced. To quote William James, "The words 'mysticism' and 'mystical' are often used as terms of mere reproach, to throw at any opinion which we regard as vague and vast and sentimental, and without a base in either facts or logic."[1] But as Paul Tillich pointed out, mysticism and mystery are derived from the Greek verb *muein,* which means "closing the eyes" or "closing the mouth." This means that a mystical experience is an experience that transcends the subject-object structure of seeing and that therefore cannot be adequately expressed in ordinary language belonging to that structure.

A propos of Tillich and the term *mystic,* the theologian Langdon Gilkey once related an amusing anecdote. Tillich, who liked to call himself a *nature mystic,* was visiting at a conference. Wishing to please him with lots of nature, his hosts drove him to a large, beautiful garden. Much to everyone's suprise, Tillich, refusing to get out of the car, inquired anxiously: "Are there any serpents in this garden?"

But enough of this general discussion. The label *poetic mystic*, like all labels, is not even important. I just wanted to give some indication of the direction in which I am going and also to establish a tie to the East, which, after all, has never made such a clear-cut distinction between philosophy and poetry and which abounds with so-called mysticism.

For my texts I shall restrict myself to four sections of *Thus Spoke Zarathustra*. The first is entitled "Before Sunrise." The Prologue to *Thus Spoke Zarathustra* began with Zarathustra rising at dawn and addressing the sun. Because in the course of the text he also addresses the moon and stars, we might call him a kind of cosmic figure. In "Before Sunrise," he speaks to the heaven. Here he is speaking not to something *in* the heaven such as the sun, moon, or stars, but to the heaven itself which he calls an *abyss of light*.

This section is replete with paradoxes, contradictions, with *coincidentia oppositorum*. To begin with, the heaven is addressed as an abyss of light. Abysses are not customarily *above* one, as is the heaven, nor are they full of light. Abysses are traditionally beneath one, and they are dark. An abyss of light is an extraordinary phenomenon indeed.

Zarathustra compared the heaven with gods and the godlike by saying, "Gods are shrouded by their beauty; thus you conceal your stars." Furthermore, he describes the heaven as "a dance floor for divine accidents, . . . a divine table for divine dice and dice players." And when Zarathustra sees the heaven, he trembles with godlike desires. This not only puts the heaven out of the domain of the ordinary and the naturalistic, but also Zarathustra himself. When the heaven, the abyss of light is about him, he is transformed into a figure of affirmation; in a sense difficult to articulate, he himself becomes a kind of heaven, protecting and blessing things.

> But I am one who can bless and say Yes, if only you are about me, pure and light, you abyss of light; then I carry the blessing of my Yes into all abysses. I have become one who blesses and says Yes; and I fought long for that and was a fighter that I might one day get my hands free to bless. But this is my blessing: to stand over every single thing as its own heaven, as its round roof, its azure bell, and eternal security; and blessed is he who blesses thus.
> For all things have been baptized in the well of eternity.[2]

The azure bell is an important image that recurs frequently in *Thus Spoke Zarathustra* as we shall see. To mention a few more of the coincidence of opposites, Zarathustra longs to throw himself into the heaven's height, that is his depth. To hide in the heaven's purity, that is *his* innocence. Ordinarily, innocence does not need to hide at all, let alone in the heaven's purity. What Zarathustra wants with all his will is "to *fly*, to fly up into *you*."

The rest of this section is concerned with getting beyond good and evil, compulsion, goals, and guilt. The purity of the heaven consists in the fact that things are freed from their bondage under purpose and reason.

> Over all things stands the heaven Accident, the heaven Innocence, the heaven Chance, the heaven high spirits (*Übermut*). . . .

This freedom and heavenly cheer I have placed over all
things like an azure bell when I taught that over them and
through them no 'eternal will' wills.[3]

These are ideas that occur consistently throughout all
of Nietzsche's writings. What is distinctive about this
section is the strange kinship, affinity, and would-be
identity between Zarathustra and the abyss of light, the
heaven. Both are described as the azure bell standing
over all things.

II

The next section with which I am concerned is the one
entitled "On the Great Longing." It follows immediately upon the crucially important section entitled "The
Convalescent," where Zarathustra finally conjures up
his most abysmal thought of eternal recurrence and,
overcome with unexpected nausea, collapses and stays
unconscious for seven days. His animals try to interpret
for him what has happened to him and who he is. But
Zarathustra does not really listen to them and we are
told that he was lying still with his eyes closed, "like one
sleeping, although he was not asleep; for he was convers-
ing with his soul."

We learn that after the confrontation with his most
abysmal thought his soul has in a way become all things,
but in a way that goes beyond Aristotle's similar sound-
ing statement. His soul is beyond all disparateness of time
and space, beyond all clouds (good and evil), and sin.

O my soul, I taught you to say "today" and "one day"
and "formerly" and to dance away over all Here and

There and Yonder. . . .

With the storm that is called "spirit" I blew over your wavy sea; I blew all clouds away; I even strangled the strangler that is called "sin." . . .

O my soul, now there is not a soul anywhere that would be more loving and comprehensive and encompassing. Where could future and past dwell closer together than in you?[4]

This soul, which is nothing "eternal" and unchangeable, Zarathustra has shaped and set free from old values, and he is now ready to baptize it with new names.

O my soul, I took from you all obeying, knee-bending, and "Lord"-saying; I myself gave you the name "turning of need" and "destiny."

O my soul, I gave you new names and colorful toys; I called you "destiny" and "circumference of circumferences" and "umbilical cord of time" and "azure bell."[5]

We have basically four new names for Zarathustra's soul. *The azure bell*, which in the section previously discussed characterized the heaven, now names Zarathustra's soul and explicitly indicates the close affinity, if not identity, between his soul and the heaven.

The circumference of circumferences has the same imagery as in the previous quote from this section, comprehensive and encompassing. The soul reaches out and around to embrace all things, not just symbolically, but quite "literally."

The umbilical cord of time is a new image characterizing time thus transmuted (future and past dwelling closest together in Zarathustra's soul) as a nourishing link to the source of life. Instead of being a principle of impermanence and finitude, this transformed time gathers all things together at the source.

Finally, Zarathustra's soul is called *destiny* and *turning of need*. Destiny is a key concept in Nietzsche's thinking that gets its fullest expression in the recurrent phrase *amor fati*, love of fate, which intentionally echoes Spinoza's *amor dei*, love of God. Turning of need (*Wende der Not*), which Kaufmann mistranslates as cessation of need, is a play on the word for necessity (*Notwendigkeit*) that distances necessity from any kind of determinism and freshly reinterprets it as turning a need (*Not*) around to work for you. It is a conception of fate, destiny, and necessity not as something outside or above us to which we are subject, but as something *within* us, as our innermost being.

III

The third section to be discussed is entitled "At Noon." In general, the seasons of the year and also the times of the day or night play an important role for Nietzsche. In the section entitled "On Involuntary Bliss," Zarathustra speaks repeatedly of the "afternoon of his life," the hour when all light grows quieter. The section "Before Sunrise" has already been discussed. And an entire book is named by the time of day: *Dawn of Day* or *Daybreak*. Probably the two most important times for Nietzsche are noon and midnight. Midnight will be discussed in the last section of *Thus Spoke Zarathustra* to be considered here.

Nietzsche's *Nachlass* is replete with sketches and plans for future works. Many of these sketches have the recurring phrase "noon and eternity." There is a sense in which noon is not really a time of day at all, but rather

out of time, timelessness, eternity. Timelessness is precisely what Zarathustra experiences in the section "At
Noon." He decides to lie down beside an old crooked
and knotty tree that was embraced by a grapevine from
which hung yellow grapes in abundance. The colors yellow and especially gold are linked with eternity; the
grapes remind us of Dionysos. Zarathustra falls asleep,
but when he speaks to his heart we are told that sleep left
his eyes open, and his soul awake. Apart from Zarathustra's description of his state, we know that it was one in
which no time elapsed because when he got up again the
sun still stood straight over his head, at exactly the place
where it was when he lay down. With characteristic levity, Nietzsche defuses the pathos of this experience of
timelessness by quipping: "But from this one might
justly conclude that Zarathustra had not slept long." The
fact that Zarathustra gets up from his resting place at the
tree as from a strange drunkenness again evokes the
Dionysian. The German word for "strange" here, *fremd*,
indicates that Zarathustra has been in a state completely
foreign and other to his normal way of experiencing.

Zarathustra begins speaking to his heart during this
state by saying:

> Still! Still! Did not the world become perfect just now?
> What is happening to me? . . . O happiness! O happiness!
> Would you sing, O my soul? You are lying in the grass.
> But this is the secret solemn hour when no shepherd
> plays his pipe. Refrain! Hot noon sleeps in the meadows.
> Do not sing! Still! the world is perfect.[6]

Many of the sections of *Thus Spoke Zarathustra* end
with the phrase: Thus spoke Zarathustra. The three song

sections, "The Night Song," "The Dancing Song," and "The Tomb Song" end with the phrase: Thus sang Zarathustra. For Nietzsche, singing is a higher expression than speaking; music is more profound than words. But in the passage just quoted, the experince goes even beyond singing. His soul wants to sing, but Zarathustra restrains it. The world has become perfect. The only appropriate response to this "perfection" is utter stillness. Nietzsche's use of the word *perfection* echoes that of an earlier thinker with whom he felt considerable affinity: Spinoza. The important thing to note here is that by perfection neither Spinoza nor Nietzsche understand an *ideal type* or *model*. We are accustomed to think, for example, of a perfect human body as an ideal type that we then use as a criterion to judge actual, individual bodies. Spinoza explicitly argues against this usage, stating that it boils down to making perfection and imperfection "really only modes of thought, that is to say, notions which we are in the habit of forming from the comparison with one another of individuals of the same species or genus."[7] Quite to the contrary, for Spinoza, as for Nietzsche, "By reality and perfection I understand the same thing."[8]

I do not wish to pursue this issue further, because that would entail a discussion of Spinoza's adamant rejection of teleology, a stance, moreover, that he also shares with Nietzsche. Suffice it to say that when Nietzsche says the world has become perfect, he means it has become totally *real*. What does that mean? We must try to interpret the rest of this section to see if some clarity can be gained as to what Nietzsche meant when he said the world had become perfect; that is, completely real.

What happened to me? Listen! Did time perhaps fly away? Do I not fall? Did I not fall—listen!—into the well of eternity? What is happening to me? Still! I have been stung, alas—in the heart? In the heart! Oh break, break, heart, after such happiness, after such a sting. How? Did not the world become perfect just now? . . . Leave me alone! Still! Did not the world become perfect just now?[9]

Zarathustra has fallen out of time into the well of eternity. When he says, Do I not fall? Did I not fall? he has left behind the distinction of past and present. Whereas previously he had wanted to *fly* up into the *abyss* of light (the heaven), now he *falls* into the *well* of eternity. Both flying and falling entail a shift of dimension, an abrupt transition to another level or realm. The abruptness is expressed in Zarathustra's words: I have been stung in the heart! A sudden sting may be linked with the image of the lightning flash (*Blitz*) which occurs repeatedly in *Thus Spoke Zarathustra* and in the *Nachlass* sketches and plans for future works. A sudden sting or lightning flash stings or strikes him all at once, vehemently transforming the person struck. The image of the lightning flash is also to be found in Meister Eckhart.

If this birth [of the son in me] has really happened, then all creatures cannot hinder you; rather they all direct you to God and to this birth, for which we have an image in the lightning flash: whatever the lightning flash hits when it strikes, be it a tree or an animal or a human being, it turns around toward itself on the spot; and if a man had turned his back, in the same instant it would hurl him around to face it.[10]

Zarathustra tries to get up, falls asleep again, and finally succeeds in waking up. At the conclusion of this whole experience he again speaks to his soul.

"Who are you? O my soul!" (At this point he was startled, for a sunbeam fell from the sky onto his face.) "O heaven over me" he said, sighing, and sat up. "You are looking on? You are listening to my strange soul? When will you drink this drop of dew which has fallen upon all earthly things? When will you drink this strange soul? When, well of eternity? Cheerful, dreadful abyss of noon! When will you drink my soul back into yourself?"[11]

Here Zarathustra is forced to ask who his soul is, even though in previous sections he has had extensive conversations with it. His soul seems to be utterly unfathomable. Again, we find kindred sentiments in Meister Eckhart.

A master who spoke of the soul best of all says that the whole of human knowledge never penetrates to know what the soul is in its ground. (To comprehend) what the soul is requires supernatural knowledge. After all, we know nothing about how the energies go out from the soul into works; perhaps we know a little about it, but that is little. No one knows anything about what the soul is in its ground.[12]

What we assume we know and are is totally unknown. Zarathustra is abruptly startled as a sunbeam falls from the heaven onto his face. He has quite literally been touched by the heaven whom he now addresses. The heaven is the well of eternity, the abyss of noon (the abyss of light). In a situation like this Nietzsche's philosophy of the will and the Will to Power simply has no place. The will, which is the great liberator from bondage and all obstacles, can do nothing here. It is not so much the case that the will is *unable* to do anything; rather *there is* nothing for it to do. To give a feeble analogy that echoes the Zarathustra section (and, strictly speaking, there are no analogies to this kind of situation; it is always unique), when there is a beautiful sunrise, "willing" is inappropriate. There is nothing to will. One can perhaps only hope to be allowed to participate in it, to be a part of it. This has nothing to do with Schopenhauer's will-less contemplation. It is more a matter of learning all things.

> To learn the Buddha Way is to learn one's self. To learn one's self is to forget one's self. To forget one's self is to be confirmed by all dharmas [all things]. To be confirmed by all dharmas is to effect the casting off of one's own body and mind and the bodies and minds of others as well. All traces of enlightenment (then) disappear, and this traceless enlightenment is continued on and on endlessly.[13]

IV

The last section to be discussed is "The Drunken Song." It is now midnight, presumably the dead opposite of noon. Midnight is more mysterious than noon; above all, it is more explicitly Dionysian. This Dionysian quality makes it impossible to simply say that noon and midnight are opposites. Otherwise one would have to try to assert that noon was Apollonian in character, going back to Nietzsche's initial primordial vision that informed and inspired all of his later works in varying degrees.

Noon and midnight are neither opposites, nor are they identical. Perhaps one could venture to say that they form a *coincidentia oppositorum*, a coincidence of opposites, a *falling together* of opposites, which is the literal and pregnant meaning of the word *coincidence*.

At the beginning of the episode we are told that "Zarathustra stood there like a drunkard." This whole experience that now begins is one of *hearing* and *smell*. The customary, overwhelmingly prevalent mode of experiencing, that of seeing, is conspicuously absent. Nothing is seen. The dualistic subject-object structure of experiencing involved in seeing falls away. No object is involved in the experience of hearing. We hear sounds, not objects. We smell odors, not objects.

Zarathustra seems to be hearing something. Everything becomes quiet and secret around him. The German word for secret, *heimlich*, literally means homelike, further strengthening and intensifying the nondualistic quality of what is to come. "Then it grew still more quiet and secret, and everything listened, even the ass and Zarathustra's animals of honor, the eagle and the serpent, as well as Zarathustra's cave and the big cool moon and the night itself."[14]

Everything is listening, even the moon and the night itself. What do they hear? From the depth comes the sound of a bell, the midnight bell "which has experienced more than any man." Now we are not only out of the dualistic subject-object structure of experiencing; we are also outside of all anthropomorphic preconceptions. The midnight bell goes beyond ordinary human experience.

The paragraphs that follow are each punctuated by a line of the song that had already appeared in Part Three at the end of the section entitled "The Other Dancing Song," and it appears again at the end of this section in its entirety, bearing the name "once more" and "into all eternity."

> O man, take care!
> What does the deep midnight declare?
> From a deep dream I woke:
> The world is deep,
> Deeper than any had thought,
> Deep is its pain—
> Joy—deeper yet than the heart's suffering:
> Pain speaks: Pass away!
> But all joy wants eternity—
> Wants deep, deep eternity![15]

Now there begins, what, for lack of more specific and concrete terms, one might call a Dionysian experience of eternity. "Where is time gone? Have I not sunk into deep wells? The world sleeps. Alas! Alas! The dog howls, the moon shines. Sooner would I die, die rather than tell you what my midnight heart thinks now. Now I have died. It is gone. Spider, what do you spin around me?"[16]

Zarathustra has sunk into the deep wells of eternity. The use of wells as plural may indicate that *well* is some kind of metaphor not to be taken too literally and not to be "localized" and objectified. The howling dog, the shining moon, and the spider all occurred together in Part Three in the crucial section entitled "On the Vision and the Enigma." Perhaps in this section the enigma is trying to become pure vision, to the extent that this is at all possible.

A turning point is indicated with the lines: "Now I have died. It is gone." What is gone and in what sense has

Zarathustra died? We learn what is gone further on in the section. "Gone! Gone! O youth! O noon! O afternoon! Now evening has come and night and midnight." In what sense has Zarathustra died? What has died is his extreme, almost inexplicable hesitation to experience midnight.

Zarathustra hears the sounds of the midnight old bell and sweet lyre. Now the sense of smell comes upon the scene, "a smell is secretly welling up, a fragrance and smell of eternity." The sense of smell is perhaps the most *intimate* sense. I must *breathe in* the odor, it has to become a part of me. The sense of smell seems to be somehow suited to transpose us directly out of ordinary time. Proust pointed out the fact that a certain odor can immediately and most vividly bring the past back to us, not as a "memory," but as a direct experience. Here Zarathustra is transposed, not into the past, but into eternity itself.

Zarathustra asks the higher men, who do not seem able to understand much of what is going on, who he is. "Am I soothsayer, a dreamer, a drunkard? An interpreter of dreams? A midnight bell? A drop of dew? A haze and fragrance of eternity? Do you not hear it? Do you not smell it? Just now my world became perfect; midnight too is noon."[17]

How can Zarathustra now say that midnight too is noon? This is the last question to be touched upon in this chapter. Again, one could be tempted to hear in the opposition of noon to midnight echoes of Nietzsche's fundamental vision of Apollo and Dionysus. Noon is the time of the brightest day, consciousness, and individuality. There are no shadows; everything is separate and distinct. Midnight is the time of primordial oneness and unity; nothing is separate and distinct. But this will not work. The experience of noon is not an Apollonian experience; it, too, is Dionysian. At noon the world also became perfect. The abyss of noon was also the well of eternity. The section "At Noon" concluded with Zarathustra asking when the abyss of noon, the well of eternity, would drink his soul back into itself.

Noon and midnight are opposites. Now we are told that they are the same. But this "sameness" is not just a dead, flat, static identity. Opposites coincide (*coincidentia oppositorum*). Midnight too is noon. Both are experiences of the well of eternity. But in the noon experience Zarathustra retains something of his own separate individuality and identity, something egolike. The experience is somewhat incomplete in that it is at the same time an anticipation, a taste of what is to come. Zarathustra asks when the well of eternity *will* drink his soul back into itself. In the midnight experience Zarathustra *becomes*, in the present moment, "a drunken sweet lyre, an ominous bell-frog that nobody understands but that *must* speak, before the deaf." Out of this experience he then speaks of woe that wants heirs and joy, which is deeper than woe, that wants itself. In other words, speaking out of the present experience of eternity, he tries to interpret eternity, to say what it means and what follows from it. We learn that joy wants *every thing*, woe included, back. This is Zarathustra's, and Nietzsche's, statement of the ultimate affirmation of life.

Apart from the reference to Dogen, this chapter has not made an explicit comparison of Nietzsche with Eastern thought. It has attempted to select some strains of Nietzsche's thought that are most consonant with an

Eastern temper of experience and to let the reader reach his own conclusions about parallels and affinities. The fact that Nietzsche's own understanding of Eastern thought was pretty well mutilated by the influence of Schopenhauer does not facilitate seeing or understanding these affinities. In particular, Buddhism gets lumped together with Christianity and both pronounced "religions of exhaustion." Temperamentally, Nietzsche was perhaps closest to Lao Tzu and Chuang Tzu with his rejection of metaphysical backworlds and his understanding of the world as play.

Notes

Chapter One. Nietzsche Today

1. *The Will to Power*, trans. Walter Kaufmann (New York: Random House, 196), nr. 820–821.

2. *Ecce Homo*, trans. Clifton Fadiman, in *The Philosopohy of Nietzsche* (New York: Random House, 1954), p. 913.

Chapter Three. Life Without Music

1. *Das Leben ohne Musik ist ein Irrtum, eine Strapaze, ein Exil.*

2. *Critique of Judgement*, trans. J. H. Bernard, p. 53.

3. *The Philosophy of Fine Art in Philosophies of Art and Beauty*, eds. Hofstadter and Kuhns (New York, 1964), p. 398.

4. *Ecce Homo*, "The Birth of Tragedy."

5. *Human All Too Human*, II, 134.

6. Nietzsche busied himself early (1870–1871) with the question of rhythm when he distinguished Greek from modern rhythm. He characterized Greek rhythm as time rhythm, as quantitative with no ictus. Modern rhythm he described as affect rhythm based upon accent.

7. *The Case of Wagner*, trans. Walter Kaufmann (New York, 1967), p. 172. The German word for actor (*Schauspieler*) expresses more forcefully the *visual* component in acting.

8. Ibid., p. 177.
9. See *The Will to Power*, nr. 849.
10. Ibid., nr. 843.
11. Ibid., nr. 845.
12. Ibid., nr. 846.
13. *The Case of Wagner*, nr. 948. Cf "The sensibility of romantic-Wagnerian music: antithesis of classical sensibility."
14. Ibid., nr. 803.
15. Ibid., nr. 842.
16. *The Philosophy of Fine Art*, Hegel, p. 392.
17. Ibid., nr. 795.
18. *Werke* XII, 214 (1883).

Chapter Four. Thoughts on Pity and Revenge

1. Stambaugh, *Nietzsche's Thought of Eternal Return* (Lanham, Md.: University Press of America, 1988); also *The Problem of Time in Nietzsche*, trans. John F. Humphrey (Lewisburg, Pa.: Bucknell University Press, 1987).

Chapter Five. Thoughts on a *Nachlass* Fragment

1. *Kritische Gesamtausgabe* V 2, p. 403.
2. *Kritische Gesamtausgabe* V 2, p. 402.
3. Spinoza, *Ethics*, III, Definition II.
4. Blake, *Auguries of Innocence*.
5. With the exception of wonder, which has no connection with anything else (Spinoza, *Ethics*, III, Definition IV).
6. *Kröner Ausgabe* II, p. 453 (author's translation).
7. Walter Kaufmann, *The Portable Nietzsche (Twilight of the Idols)*, p. 485.
8. *Nachlass, The Will to Power* (1887–1888), trans. Walter Kaufmann, p. 1035.
9. Ibid. (1887), p. 712.

10. Ibid. (1887), p. 1037.

11. Ibid. (1887), p. 639.

12. *Beyond Good and Evil*, trans. H. Zimmern (New York: Modern Library, 1954), p. 150.

13. See, for example, *Zarathustha* III, *Before Sunrise*.

Chapter Six. *Amor dei* and *Amor fati*: Spinoza and Nietzsche

1. Baruch Spinoza, *Ethics*, I, prop. XVII.

2. Ibid., prop. XXXIV.

3. Ibid., III, prop. XIII.

4. Ibid., def. II

5. The last line of Sophocles' *Oedipus at Colonus*, usually rendered "For all this is determined," could also be read, "For all this is perfected."

6. *Ethics*, II, def. 6, IV, Preface.

7. Ibid., I, prop. XXXIV.

8. Ibid., V, prop. XXXII, corollary (trans. William Hale White, rev. Amelia Hutchinson Sterling, 4th ed., rev. and corr. [London: H. Frouder, 1910]).

9. Ibid., prop. XXXVI.

10. See *Nietzsche contra Wagner*, Epilogue; *Ecce Homo*, "Why I Write Such Good Books"; *The Case of Wagner*, sec. 4.

11. S, sec. 61 (author's translation).

12. *Ecce Homo*, "Why I Am So Wise," trans. Fadiman, sec. 6.

13. *The Will to Power*, trans. Kaufmann, sec. 243.

14. Ibid., sec. 1041.

15. *Zarathustra*, II, "On Redemption," trans. Kaufmann.

16. *Ecce Homo*, "Why I Am So Clever," author's translation, sec. 10.

17. *Zarathustra*, III, "On the Great Longing," trans. Kaufmann.

18. Ibid., "Before Sunrise," trans. Kaufmann.

19. Ibid.

20. *Zarathustra*, IV, "At Noon," trans. Kaufmann.

21. Ibid.

22. *Ethics*, V, prop. XXXVI.

23. *The Will to Power*, trans. Kaufmann, sec. 55.

24. GOA, XIII, p. 63.

25. GOA, XIV, p. 99.

Chapter Seven. The Innocence of Becoming

1. *Kritische Gesamtausgabe*, VII, 3, 385.

2. *Zarathustra*, IV, "Retired" (*Ausser Dienst*), in *The Portable Nietzsche*.

3. *Zarathustra*, IV, "The Ugliest Man" (*Der hässlichste Mensch*), trans. Walter Kaufmann.

4. *Zarathustra*, III, "Before Sunrise" (*Vor Sonnen-Aufgang*).

5. Ibid.

6. Ibid.

7. Cf. *Kritische Gesamtausgabe*, VIII, 2, 281 (author's translation).

8. *The Use and Disadvantage of History for Life*, I, (HL 1), trans. Peter Preuss (Indianapolis, In.: Hackett, 1980).

9. Ibid.

10. Ibid.

11. Ibid.

12. *Untimely Meditations*, III, 5 (*Unzeitgemässe Betrachtungen* III 5), trans. Peter Preuss.

13. *Zarathustra*, I, "The Three Metamorphoses" (*Von den drei Verwandlungen*), trans. Walter Kaufmann.

14. *The Will to Power* 797, trans. Walter Kaufmann and R. J. Hollingdale (New York: Random House, 1967).

15. *Zarathustra*, II, "On Immaculate Perception" (*Von der unbefleckten Erkenntnis*), trans. Walter Kaufmann.

16. *Beyond Good and Evil*, (JGB 150), trans. Walter Kaufmann, p. 150.

17. *The Will to Power* 765, trans. Walter Kaufmann and R. J. Hollingdale.

18. *Ecce Homo, Warum ich so klug bin*, trans. Walter Kaufmann, p. 10.

19. *Kritische Gesamtausgabe*, VIII, 1, 148.

20. *Kritische Gesamtausgabe*, VII, 1, 649.

21. *Kritische Gesamtausgabe*, VII, 1, 540 and VII, 2, 292.

Chapter Eight. Appearance: Nihilism or Affirmation

1. *Twilight of the Idols* in *The Portable Nietzsche*, pp. 485–486.

2. *The Will to Power*, paragraphs 2 and 3.

3. *The Gay Science*, trans. Walter Kaufmann (New York: Random House, 1974).

4. *Twilight of the Idols*, trans. R. J. Hollingdale (Baltimore: Penguin Books, 1968), p. 36.

5. *The Will to Power*, nr. 822.

6. Ibid., nr. 585.

7. *Beyond Good and Evil*, trans. Zimmern, p. 34.

8. *The Will to Power*, nr. 585.

9. Intoxication; the psychological condition of the artist.

10. *Twilight of the Idols*, trans. Kaufmann, p. 72.

11. Ibid., p. 54.

12. *The Will to Power*, nr. 846.

13. Schopenhauer's parody of Leibniz's "this is the best of all possible worlds."

14. *The Birth of Tragedy*.

15. *The Will to Power*, nr. 853.

Chapter Nine. The Other Nietzsche

1. William James, *Varieties of Religious Experience* (New York: Modern Library), p. 370.

2. *Thus Spoke Zarathustra*,"Before Sunrise," *The Portable Nietzsche*, pp. 277–278.

3. Ibid., p. 278 with minor changes.

4. Ibid., "The Great Longing," pp. 333–334.

5. Ibid., p. 334.

6. Ibid., "At Noon," p. 388.

7. Spinoza, *Ethics* IV, Preface.

8. Ibid., II, Def. VI.

9. Op. cit., p. 389.

10. Meister Eckehart, *Deutsche Predigten und Traktate* (München: Carl Hanser Verlag, 1955), p. 437.

11. Op. cit., "At Noon," p. 390.

12. Meister Eckhart, op. cit., p. 190.

13. *The Eastern Buddhist*, vol. 5, no. 2, trans. Norman Waddell and Masao Abe, pp. 134–135.

14. Op. cit., "The Drunken Song," p. 431.

15. Ibid., p. 436.

16. Ibid., p. 432.

17. Ibid., p. 435.

Index